Born Again

Theological Reflections on Evangelism and Grace

Jonathan Vorce

Jonathan Vorce Ministries Inc.

Born Again

Theological Reflections on Evangelism and Grace

Copyright © 2024 by Jonathan Vorce

Scripture quotations taken from:

The Holy Bible, New International Version® NIV®

Copyright © 1973, 1978, 1984, 2011 by Biblica, Inc.

Used with permission. All rights reserved worldwide.

The Holy Bible, English Standard Version ® ESV

Copyright © 2001 by Crossway, a publishing ministry of

Good News Publishers. Used by permission.

The New King James Version® NKJV®

Scripture taken from the New King James Version®. Copyright © 1982 by Thomas Nelson. Used by permission. All rights reserved.

King James Version (KJV), public domain.

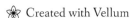

Contents

Introduction

Evangelism, the dissemination of the gospel's message of redemption to a world in dire need, remains a subject of paramount importance to God. His profound affection for humanity was encapsulated in the act of giving, as articulated in John 3:16, where it is states,

> *"For God so loved the world, that he gave his only begotten Son, that whosoever believeth in him should not perish, but have everlasting life."* ~ John 3:16

The truth of the gospel, expressed by D. L. Moody, underscores the depth of love conveyed in the term 'so,' highlighting God's divine concern for individuals ensnared in sin and suffering.

The landscape of evangelism has witnessed a resurgence of interest in recent years. This renewed focus transcends doctrinal divides. Notably, the impetus provided by figures such as Billy Graham has led to the organization of world congresses dedicated to this cause. Furthermore, the emphasis on evangelistic ministry has permeated various conventions, denominational assemblies, and parish conferences, eliciting commendation for all earnest endeavors in this field.

Despite this burgeoning interest, contemporary discussions on evangelism often overlook crucial theological underpinnings essential for a comprehensive understanding of the subject. While current dialogues may touch upon certain doctrinal aspects, they frequently neglect core biblical principles such as divine sovereignty, human incapacity, and the transformative power of grace. These elements are not merely ancillary; they are foundational to the practice of evangelism. The omission of these themes represents a significant oversight, as evangelism cannot be reduced to mere methodological considerations. Indeed, authentic evangelistic efforts spring from a well-grounded theological framework.

In summary, the essence of evangelism lies not in the mechanics of its execution but in the theological convictions that fuel it. Acknowledging and integrating foundational doctrines such as the sovereignty of God, the limitations of human agency, and the efficacy of divine grace is imperative for the effective communication of the gospel. Evangelism, therefore, is intrinsically linked to a robust theological foundation, underscoring the necessity of revisiting and reinforcing these core principles within contemporary evangelical discourse.

Chapter 1

Defining Evangelism

E vangelism is a key aspect of the Christian faith, but it can often be misunderstood or even controversial. In simple terms, evangelism refers to sharing the good news of Jesus Christ with others and inviting them to become followers of Him. It is seen as a fundamental responsibility for Christians to spread the message of God's love and salvation to those who have not yet heard it. So, what exactly does evangelism entail and why is it so important? This chapter seeks to answer these questions and more.

At its core, evangelism involves the dissemination of a divine message to non-believers. The word "evangelism" derives from the Greek word for gospel, meaning "good news." This good news refers to the message of salvation through Jesus Christ and his death and resurrection. Therefore, at its core, evangelism is about sharing this good news with those who have not yet heard it or accepted it.

The Divine Origin of the Gospel

In apostolic times, Paul was a principal figure in preaching the gospel, amidst challenges from Judaizers who sought to dilute its purity with extraneous elements. His teachings serve to illuminate the divine origin of the gospel, distinguishing it from human contrivances aimed at addressing humanity's existential dilemmas. Paul's assertions in Galatians 1:11-12 emphasize the gospel's heavenly genesis, received through the revelation of Jesus Christ. This divine origination underscores its immutable and definitive character, setting it apart from all other religious propositions. Anyone found altering the gospel's message was met with the gravest of condemnations, highlighting its sacrosanct nature.

In contemporary ecumenical contexts, the pursuit of dialogue among various world religions often involves comparisons and attempts to find common theological grounds. However, the gospel of Christ stands unique in its divine inception, unmatched by any other religious system's humanly constructed doctrines. This uniqueness mandates that believers advocate the gospel with the same exclusivity and conviction as Paul, recognizing it as an unrivaled divine message.

The Divine Authority of the Gospel

The apostolic proclamation of the gospel was imbued with divine authority, as evidenced by the preaching of the apostles "with the Holy Ghost sent down from heaven" (1 Peter 1:12). This manner of preaching transcended mere academic or philosophical discourse, embodying a declarative and commanding presentation of the truth. The apostles' preaching was marked by certainty and boldness, reflecting their unwavering belief in the divine backing of their message[^3].

Contemporary evangelical approaches occasionally diverge from this paradigm, adopting methods perceived as more palatable to modern sensibilities, such as sharing, discussing, and engaging in dialogue. While these techniques may incorporate valuable elements, there is concern that they may dilute the robust, authoritative nature of gospel proclamation as exemplified in the apostolic era. The shift towards a more apologetic and softened form of evangelism risks compromising the gospel's inherent authority in an attempt to accommodate contemporary attitudes[^4].

Therefore, evangelism, as delineated in the New Testament, is the propagation of a message with a divine origin and authority. This understanding is crucial for faithfully communicating the gospel, ensuring that its presentation remains true to its sacred source and is conveyed with the conviction befitting its divine mandate.

The Transformative Power of the Gospel

At the commencement of his profound exposition on the divine plan for human salvation, Paul asserts with conviction that the gospel embodies "the power of God unto salvation" (Romans 1:16). This declaration underscores the intrinsic potency of the gospel, attributed to the omnipotence of God imbued within its message.

Salvation Story

Evangelist Billy Graham's conversion experience is a seminal event that shaped not only his personal spiritual trajectory but also had profound implications for Christian evangelism in the 20th century. Graham's encounter with faith was not marked by dramatic visions or miraculous signs; instead, it was deeply personal and rooted in the human experience of seeking purpose and meaning. In 1934, during a series of revival meetings in Charlotte, North Carolina, led by evangelist Mordecai Ham, Graham, then a teenager, felt a compelling tug at his heart. Despite his initial reluctance and the skepticism he harbored, the message of grace, redemption, and personal commitment to Jesus Christ spoke to him on a profound level. He made the decision to accept Jesus into his life, a moment of spiritual awakening that he described as filling him with an overwhelming sense of peace and purpose.*

This pivotal event unfolded in an atmosphere of fervent prayer and intense spiritual yearning, characteristic of the revivalist tradition within which it took place. Graham's conversion did not occur in isolation but within the community of believers, underscoring the importance of communal faith practices and the support of the faithful in the Christian tradition. It laid the foundation for his future ministry, which would be characterized by an unyielding commitment to preaching the Gospel and a deep conviction in the transformative power of faith. Billy Graham went on to become one of the most influential Christian leaders of his time, preaching to millions around the world and bringing the message of faith to the furthest corners of the earth. His conversion serves as a testament to the power of personal faith and the impact of spiritual awakening on an individual's life and the world at large.

The essence and ultimate aim of the gospel are encapsulated succinctly in the phrase "unto salvation." It presents a narrative not just of theoretical or moral guidance but of a dynamic force capable of fundamentally altering human existence. The gospel extends beyond offering mere philosophical insights or ethical guidelines; it provides individuals who are ensnared in a state of

---

* The Billy Graham Evangelistic Association, "Billy Graham's Life and Ministry

despair and hopelessness with an opportunity for profound transformation and eternal hope through Jesus Christ.

This message, heralded by believers, is not of mundane origin but is described as the "glorious gospel of the blessed God" (1 Timothy 1:11), emphasizing its divine roots and the unparalleled splendor it carries. Such a proclamation does not merely suggest a path to self-improvement but announces the availability of a new life and lasting hope grounded in Christ's redemptive work.

In essence, the gospel's power is not confined to the parameters of human intellect or achievement; it is a testament to the boundless capability of divine intervention in the human condition. Through the gospel, individuals are invited not just to amend their lives but to undergo a radical transformation, enabling them to attain salvation and experience the fullness of life envisioned by God.

Therefore, the gospel stands as a beacon of divine power, offering salvation and a renewed existence to all who embrace its truth. Its message transcends ordinary human discourse, encapsulating the profound impact of God's omnipotence in bringing about salvation and hope to humanity.

The Presentation of a Divine Person

Evangelism, at its core, is the act of sharing the gospel, which fundamentally revolves around the revelation of Jesus Christ. This proclamation is not just about disseminating information; it's about presenting a divine being—Christ Himself—as elucidated in "the gospel of the glory of Christ" (2 Corinthians 4:4). The essence of evangelism is to unveil the magnificence of Christ, ensuring that nothing detracts from His splendor or obstructs the view of Him to the world. It transcends the promotion of personal achievements, church expansions, or program endorsements, focusing solely on the personhood and mission of Jesus Christ, who embarked on a redemptive mission to save humanity from sin.

The Gospel of the Eternal Christ

Paul, in the foundational text of Romans, delineates three pivotal truths about the gospel's relation to Jesus Christ. Firstly, the "gospel of God" (Romans 1:1) centers on "His Son" (Romans 1:3), described as the "Son of God with power" (Romans 1:4). These titles signify Christ's eternal nature rather than suggesting a temporal beginning. Contrary to interpretations by some groups like Jehovah's Witnesses, the New Testament's reference to Christ as the "Son" illuminates His perpetual relationship with the Father, negating any notion of temporal genesis. Scriptures such as "Thou art my Son; this day have I begotten thee" (Psalms 2:7; cf. Hebrews 1:5) speak to Christ's eternal coexistence and equality with the Father, portraying Him as the timeless "I am" (John 8:58), without beginning or end, who conquered death to reign eternally (Revelation 1:18).

The Gospel of the Incarnate Christ

Furthermore, Paul articulates the incarnation of Christ, stating He "was made of the seed of David according to the flesh" (Romans 1:3). This profound mystery of the eternal Christ taking on human form underscores the imperative for God's intervention in human history. The incarnation allowed for the divine to intimately engage with humanity, facilitating a bridge to salvation. The eternal Son's assumption of humanity did not diminish His divinity; instead, it heralded the unique union of God and man within one entity—Jesus Christ. This union was essential for overcoming death and the dominion of evil, as reflected in "through death he might destroy him that had the power of death, that is, the devil" (Hebrews 2:14). Without this incarnate presence, the foundation of the gospel and the very act of evangelism would be void.

Evangelism, therefore, is a testament to the divine narrative encapsulated in the life, death, and resurrection of Jesus Christ. It invites individuals to encounter the Divine through the person of Christ, offering salvation and an eternal relationship with God. This divine mission is not a mere historical event but a continuing invitation to experience transformation and hope through the gospel's message.

The Gospel of the Resurrected Christ

The pivotal message of the gospel centers on Jesus Christ, who was "declared to be the Son of God with power... by his resurrection from the dead" (Romans 1:4). In the realm of evangelism, acknowledging the resurrection of Christ is paramount[^1]. The essence of the gospel does not reside in the teachings of a deceased mentor but in the dynamic presence of a living Savior who triumphed over death, extending salvation to all who accept this truth. Christ's representation is not as one perpetually affixed to the cross; rather, He is celebrated and worshipped as one who lives.

This element of resurrection is consistently emphasized in apostolic sermons documented within the Acts of the Apostles, underscoring its critical role both as a compelling defense of the faith and a core component of the evangelical message[^2]. The resurrection of Christ is more than a historical event; it serves as a testament to His divine authority and ability to liberate humanity from sin.

Evangelistic preaching is intrinsically linked to the person of

Jesus Christ. Authentic evangelism is characterized by its capacity to elevate Christ in such a manner that individuals are confronted with His majesty and prompted to place their faith in Him[^3]. In essence, the proclamation of the gospel is an invitation to recognize and respond to the glory of the resurrected Christ, offering individuals a pathway to redemption and eternal life.

Divine Intervention for Humanity

The gospel represents not merely a call to human endeavor but a divine message meant to be received with faith. This was articulated by Paul when he outlined the core of the gospel message, emphasizing the sacrificial death and resurrection of Christ as foundational truths anchored in scripture: "For I delivered unto you first of all that which I also received, how that Christ died for our sins according to the scriptures; and that he was buried, and that he rose again the third day according to the scriptures" (1 Corinthians 15:3-4). This passage illuminates the gospel's nature, revealing it as a divine initiative for humanity's redemption.

A Substitutionary Work

At the heart of Paul's declaration is the concept of substitution —Christ's death on behalf of humanity. The preposition "for" conveys the idea of Jesus Christ taking our place, bearing the penalty for our transgressions. He became the substitute, shouldering the consequences of our sins.

The New Testament elucidates the doctrine of Christ's substitutionary sacrifice. We are redeemed through "the precious blood of Christ, as of a lamb without blemish and without spot" (1 Peter 1:19), underscoring the purity and value of His sacrificial death. Further, Christ is described as "the propitiation for our sins: and not for ours only, but also for the sins of the whole world" (1 John 2:2), indicating His role in appeasing the divine justice required by a holy God. Propitiation refers to Christ's death satisfying the righteous demands of God, allowing sinners who believe to be liberated from the judgment they deserved.

This concept is vividly portrayed in the prophecy of Isaiah, who foretold the suffering Messiah would be "wounded for our transgressions" and "bruised for our iniquities" (Isaiah 53:5), highlighting the vicarious nature of His suffering. Isaiah further explains that the Lord placed upon Him "the iniquity of us all" (Isaiah 53:6), symbolizing the complete transfer of humanity's sin to Christ.

These scriptural insights reveal the gospel as the proclamation of Christ's divine work on the cross—a selfless act of love whereby He took upon Himself the judgment destined for us, offering salvation and peace through His wounds. It is this profound truth that forms the bedrock of the Christian faith, inviting individuals to believe in the accomplished work of Christ for their redemption.

A Completed Work in Christian Theology

The phrase "Christ died for our sins" encapsulates the notion of a completed work, a foundational principle extensively elaborated upon throughout the New Testament. This concept of a "finished work" encompasses three critical theological components: redemption concerning sin, reconciliation towards humanity, and propitiation in relation to God.

Redemption and the Price Paid: The term "redemption" in the New Testament context implies a transaction—specifically, the payment of a price. This concept is richly illustrated through various scriptural texts, indicating that believers are redeemed "through his blood" (Ephesians 1:7). This redemption is described as a liberation from the bondage of sin, a purchase made at a great cost, highlighting the sacrificial death of Christ as the means through which humans are afforded grace and justification before God (Romans 3:23-24). The imagery of being "bought with a price" (1 Corinthians 6:20) underscores the magnitude of Christ's sacrifice, offering freedom and new life.

Reconciliation and Restored Relationship: Reconciliation addresses the estrangement between humanity and God, an alienation resulting from sin. Contrary to some interpretations, it was not God who needed to be reconciled but humanity, which had drifted away. Through Christ's death, an avenue was created for reconciling the world unto Himself, effectively bridging the gap and transforming the relationship between God and humanity (2 Corinthians 5:17-18). This transformation is poignantly depicted in hymns and scriptures alike, celebrating the restored fellowship with God, now accessible to all through faith in Christ.

Propitiation and Divine Satisfaction: Propitiation refers to the appeasement or satisfaction of God's righteous demands through Christ's sacrificial death. This aspect, along with redemption and reconciliation, constitutes the complete work of Christ, signifying the final and sufficient sacrifice for sins. Unlike the continual offerings in the Old Testament, which could never fully remove sin, Christ's single sacrifice achieved eternal perfection for believers (Hebrews 10:11-12). This marks a pivotal shift from the provisional measures of the past to the definite accomplishment of redemption, making the good news of the gospel available to all.

Salvation, therefore, is not an achievement of human endeavor but a gift from God, underscoring the totality of Christ's payment for sin. The compelling truth of the gospel lies in the complete sufficiency of Christ's sacrifice—He paid it all, leaving no debt unpaid, erasing the stain of sin and offering purity and reconciliation to those who believe.

The apostle Paul emphasizes the gospel's vital role in salvation, stating it is "by which also ye are saved" (1 Corinthians 15:2). This declaration underscores that the gospel transcends mere intellectual speculation or moral guidance; it embodies a divine and potent message capable of transforming lives. The essence of the gospel lies not in its theoretical value but in its practical efficacy and divine origin, serving as the vehicle for God's saving power.

The gospel functions as "the power of God unto salvation to everyone that believes" (Romans 1:16), illustrating its universal applicability and inherent strength. It is not merely a set of doctrines to be debated or ethical principles to be adopted but a dynamic force that brings about spiritual renewal and salvation. At the heart of this message is the redemptive work of Jesus Christ, who extends the offer of salvation to all willing to accept Him. This aspect of the gospel is crucial; it is not just about understanding or admiring the life of Christ but about embracing His sacrifice and victory over sin as the means of our own salvation.

Evangelism, therefore, is much more than conveying information; it is about sharing the living, breathing message of hope and redemption found in Christ. Through the gospel, individuals encounter the profound reality of God's love and provision for humanity, leading to transformation and new life. The gospel presents not just a path to better living but the promise of eternal life through faith in Jesus Christ.

The gospel stands as a testament to God's desire to save and transform those who believe. It is this "saving work of the Lord Jesus Christ" that remains central to the Christian faith, offering hope and redemption to a world in need.

A Divine Summons to Believe

The gospel of Christ is not a mere retelling of ancient events or an optional belief system; it is a divine summons to believe in the redemptive work of Jesus Christ and accept His free gift of salvation. The Bible states that "God was in Christ, reconciling the world unto himself" (2 Corinthians 5:19), underscoring His deep love and desire to restore the broken relationship between humanity and Himself. This divine summons is extended to all, regardless of background or status, for "whosoever will" may come (Revelation 22:17).

The Demand for Obedience to the Gospel

Contrary to some contemporary interpretations of evangelism as an exchange of religious views or a dialogue on societal issues, the biblical account, particularly by Paul, conveys a sterner message. He articulates the grave consequences awaiting those who disregard the gospel, aiming to inspire a heightened sense of duty among believers. This is vividly depicted in his letter to the Thessalonians, where he speaks of a future where "the Lord Jesus shall be revealed from heaven with his mighty angels, in flaming fire taking vengeance on them that know not God, and that obey not the gospel of our Lord Jesus Christ" (2 Thessalonians 1:7-9).

This passage underscores the seriousness with which the gospel must be received and adhered to.

Some individuals, misunderstanding the relationship between grace and faith, interpret the call to "obey not the gospel" as implying that salvation involves certain deeds or rituals. However, within the scriptural context, "obey" essentially means to "believe." To obey the gospel, then, is to accept Jesus Christ as one's savior, acknowledging the gospel's authority and submitting oneself to divine sovereignty[2]. Here, the term is deliberately chosen to highlight the gospel's ultimatum: believe or face eternal separation from God. This perspective emphasizes the gospel's inherent authority and the critical need for submission to God's directive— belief in Christ as the only path to salvation.

The Consequences of Disregarding the Gospel

The language used to describe the fate of those who ignore this call is stark and unequivocal: terms like "flaming fire," "everlasting destruction," and "from the presence of the Lord" (2 Thessalonians 1:8, 9) paint a grim picture of eternal separation from God's grace and love[3]. "Everlasting destruction" here does not imply cessation of existence but denotes a perpetual state of ruin, a condition marked by the absence of all that is good and the inability to fulfill any purpose for eternity. Such a destiny awaits those who remain unrepentant, forever excluded from the benevolent presence of the Lord, consigned to an existence devoid of hope and light.

Therefore, evangelism is defined by its urgent call to respond to the gospel—a message of salvation through faith in Jesus Christ. This proclamation bears the weight of divine authority, demanding acknowledgment and acceptance of Christ's redemptive work. It serves as a stark reminder of the serious implications of disbelief, underscoring the necessity of compliance with the gospel's call as the only means to avoid eternal separation from God.

In conclusion, The gospel of Christ is not a passive doctrine, but an active force that impels believers to share its life-changing message with others. As Christians, we are called to fulfill the Great Commission, proclaiming the good news and demonstrating its transformative power through our lives. We must heed the call to obedience and boldly declare the gospel's truth, knowing the eternal consequences for those who reject it. The gospel remains the focal point of our faith and the hope of all believers, offering salvation and new life to a lost world. Let us, therefore, continue to share this message with fervor and conviction, knowing that through the gospel, lives are transformed and eternities are changed.

Chapter 2

Theology and Evangelism

H ave you ever considered how deeply intertwined theology and evangelism are within the Christian faith? These two elements, often seen as separate entities, are, in fact, inseparably married to one another. Imagine evangelism and theology as two sides of the same coin, each incomplete without the other, each enriching and empowering the Christian mission.

In the realm of faith, it's not uncommon to witness a divide between scholars and practitioners. Some evangelists and pastors, focused intensely on action and outreach, may view theologians as distant and overly academic, engaged more with ancient languages and complex terms than with the pressing need to save souls. They might say, "Why dwell on soteriological definitions when thousands are perishing without the Gospel?"

Conversely, certain theologians and scholarly pastors gaze upon evangelistic efforts with concern, fearing a lack of depth, a focus on emotional appeal over substance—essentially, a message "full of sound and fury, signifying nothing."

But here lies a question that stirs the heart: have we forgotten that God bestows different gifts upon His children? Some are blessed with profound scholarly insight, a gift accompanied often by a temperament inclined towards study and reflection rather than dynamic public ministry. Yet, these theologians, through their dedication to understanding God's word deeply, play a crucial role in the body of Christ. They may not be the ones leading rallies or evangelistic campaigns, but in their quiet study, they are fervently serving the Lord in the way He has called them.

On the flip side, evangelists, those spirited individuals driven to action, possess a unique gift of reaching out and touching hearts, drawing people towards Christ in ways that scholars may not. Their zeal, their ability to motivate and inspire, is a divine calling that complements the reflective depth of theology.

Isn't it clear, then, that both evangelists and theologians are essential? One cannot transform an evangelist into a theologian nor a theologian into an evangelist through mere human effort or desire. Each has a vital role, a divine calling that needs to be recognized and respected.

For theology to truly resonate and impact lives, it must be "knowledge on fire" — alive, vibrant, and applied. And for evangelism to fulfill its heavenly purpose, it must be grounded in sound theology, ensuring that the message spread is one of depth and truth. The theological framework surrounding evangelism isn't merely an academic exercise; it's the foundation that supports and gives meaning to our efforts to share the Gospel.

In this beautiful dance between theology and evangelism, we find a model for our own lives. Are we not called to both deep understanding and passionate action? To live out our calling, we must seek to empower ourselves with knowledge while also stepping out in faith to share the hope within us. It's in this unity of knowledge and action that we can truly unlock our potential, living out our highest calling in Christ.

The Theology of Evangelism

When we hear the word "theology," many of us may immediately think of complex doctrines and debates among scholars. However, at its core, theology is simply the study of God and His relationship with humanity. It encompasses all aspects of our faith, from the nature of God to salvation to Christian living.

But why is it essential to consider theology when it comes to evangelism? To put it simply, the message we share through evangelism is rooted in our understanding of God and His word. If our theology is flawed or shallow, then our efforts to spread the Gospel will also be lacking.

In fact, throughout history, many heresies and false teachings have arisen due to a lack of sound theology. Without a strong foundation, it's easy for individuals to distort the message of salvation and mislead others.

On the other hand, a robust understanding of theology can greatly enhance our evangelistic efforts. When we have a deep knowledge of God and His word, we are better equipped to share the Gospel with others confidently and accurately. We can address common questions or objections from a place of understanding and offer a clear, coherent message.

Furthermore, theology can also serve as a guide for how we approach evangelism. It reminds us to share the good news out of love and compassion rather than judgment or condemnation. It encourages us to focus on the transformative power of the Gospel rather than emotional manipulation or empty rhetoric.

Ultimately, the theology of evangelism is not an abstract concept but a practical and necessary foundation for effective mission work. As Christians, it's our responsibility to study and understand God's word deeply so that we can share it effectively with others.

The Personal Nature of God

Have you ever paused to consider the true essence of God? This question may seem like something only theologians ponder, but it holds profound significance for each of us. In a world teeming with diverse beliefs and philosophies, understanding the personal nature of God is both a challenge and an adventure.

When Paul stood on Mars Hill, addressing the Athenian crowd, he wasn't just speaking into the air. He was introducing them to something revolutionary—the concept of a living, breathing, personal God[1]. This was a groundbreaking moment, especially considering that his audience was deeply entrenched in their own beliefs, unaware of the true God's nature.

God as a Person

To some, the idea of God being a person might seem obvious, especially among those who grew up in environments where this truth is regularly celebrated. However, this concept isn't as universally accepted as one might think. Today's society, heavily influenced by modern rationalism, humanism, and a plethora of philosophies, often rejects the notion of a personal deity. The rise of oriental mysticism and other worldviews in places like the United States has only added layers to this skepticism.

Yet, the essence of God's personality shines through the clutter of these beliefs. Throughout history, missionaries venturing into different cultures have encountered a myriad of perspectives on the divine—animism, pantheism, and more—each missing the mark on recognizing God's personal nature.

Paul, in his discourse in Athens, didn't shy away from declaring the truth of a personal God. (Acts 17:22-34) In this scripture passage various actions are attributed to God such as:

- Creating, v. 24
- Sustaining, v. 25
- Commanding Worship, v. 25
- Determining, v.26
- Commanding Repentance, v. 29
- Raising Christ, v. 31
- Judging the Wicked, v. 31

Therefore, Paul illustrated vividly that God is not a distant force or abstract entity. He is a person. The declaration "I AM," revealed to Moses in Exodus 3:14, encapsulates this beautifully. It speaks of God's self-consciousness, self-determination, and intimate presence among us. These are not the attributes of an impersonal force but of someone deeply personal and relational.

The Impact of Understanding God's Personality

Why does this matter to us? Because recognizing God as a person transforms how we relate to Him. It's not about adhering to rituals or following a set of philosophical ideas. It's about nurturing a relationship with a God who knows us, loves us, and desires to be involved in our lives. It shifts our perspective from seeing God as a distant overseer to understanding Him as a loving Father, a faithful friend, and a constant guide.

In this light, every prayer becomes a conversation, every scripture a letter, and every moment of worship an opportunity to connect personally with the Creator of the universe. This under-standing empowers us, motivates us, and invites us to live out our calling in a relationship with a God who is not only sovereign over the cosmos but is intimately involved in the details of our lives.

As we continue our journey, exploring the depths of faith and spirituality, may we always seek to deepen our understanding of God's personal nature. For in doing so, we unlock a more fulfilling, dynamic, and empowering walk with Him—one that truly trans-forms our lives.

God is the Supreme Architect of it ALL

In a world brimming with theories and narratives about our origins, have you ever stopped to ponder the profound implica-tions of acknowledging God as the Creator of everything that exists? This is not merely a theological assertion; it's the founda-tion upon which our understanding of morality, purpose, and accountability rests.

The declaration made in Acts 17:24, that God "made the world and all things therein," isn't just ancient text—it's the bedrock of our meaningful existence. Why? Because if we dismiss the idea of a personal God who meticulously crafted every detail of the universe, we're left drifting in a sea of moral ambiguity with no anchor of truth.

The Challenge of Evolution

Today, the theory of evolution is heralded by many as an unde-niable fact. Particularly within academic circles, challenging this narrative can often label one as outmoded or disconnected from modern scientific discourse. Yet, despite its widespread accep-tance, critical voices argue that the theory lacks concrete scientific evidence, pointing instead to the clear biblical account of divine creation as the ultimate explanation of our existence.

Why does this matter so much? If we entertain the notion that we are mere products of chance, products of a blind evolutionary process with no deliberate design or purpose, where does that leave us? Suddenly, the concept of moral accountability seems baseless. If life sprang from random events, then the very idea of a moral law, fixed and authoritative, crumbles away. We are left with a morality that is as fleeting and changeable as the circumstances that supposedly birthed us.

But, when we recognize God as the Creator, everything changes. This acknowledgment brings with it a profound sense of accountability to a higher moral authority. It's about understanding that our lives are not accidents but intentional creations by a God who has the sovereign right to guide, instruct, and demand our allegiance.

Consider this for a moment: if we are indeed created by God, intricately woven together with purpose and intention, doesn't that imbue our lives with immense value and meaning? Beyond a shadow of a doubt, it reassures us that there is an absolute moral standard, a compass that guides us through the complexities of life.

This perspective is indispensable in evangelism. It's not about promoting a religion; it's about inviting others into a relationship with a God who loves them deeply, who crafted the stars yet knows their name. It's about connecting hearts back to their Creator, helping them find their place in the grand narrative of divine creation.

In the dance between faith and reason, may we have the courage to explore beyond the surface. May we open our hearts to the possibility that we are more than cosmic accidents—that we are, indeed, creations of a purposeful, loving God. This realization empowers us to live fully, love deeply, and walk confidently in the light of His truth.

Understanding the Sovereignty of God

In a world where uncertainty often prevails, the concept of a Sovereign God stands as a beacon of hope and assurance. Imagine a deity not limited by time, space, or the myriad complexities of the universe—a God who reigns supreme over all creation. This is the God introduced by Paul on Mars Hill, described as "the Lord of heaven and earth" (Acts 17:24). Such a portrayal transcends any notion of a deity grappling with limitations or challenges within His own creation.

God's sovereignty means He is the ultimate authority and ruler, orchestrating the events of the universe in perfect harmony, according to His divine will. Unlike humans, who often find themselves at the mercy of circumstances or surprises, God is "surprised by nothing." This truth is beautifully captured in Psalms 115:3, which declares, "But our God is in the heavens: he hath done whatsoever he hath pleased." This scripture underscores the absolute freedom and power of God, affirming that everything unfolds under His sovereign will.

The Implications of Divine Sovereignty

What does this mean for us? Firstly, understanding God's sovereignty offers profound peace and comfort. In a world that sometimes feels chaotic and unpredictable, knowing that a loving, sovereign God is in control can transform our perspective on life's trials and tribulations. It reassures us that there is a purpose behind every event, even when we cannot see it.

Furthermore, recognizing God's sovereignty invigorates our mission to share His word and reach out to those who are lost. It's empowering to know that we are commissioned by a God who holds absolute authority over the universe. This doesn't just imbue our evangelistic efforts with purpose; it also provides the confidence to move forward, knowing that God is orchestrating the outcomes according to His perfect plan.

Therefore, the sovereignty of God invites us to trust Him more deeply, releasing our anxieties and doubts into His capable hands. It encourages us to pray with conviction, serve with passion, and evangelize with boldness, secure in the knowledge that God's plans are always for our good and His glory.

But it also calls us into action. Knowing that we serve a sovereign Lord, how can we not be moved to share the hope and assurance we have in Christ? How can we keep silent about a God who is actively working in the world, drawing people to Himself, and inviting everyone into a relationship with Him?

In every whisper of our hearts, in every step of faith, may we always remember the sovereignty of God. May it be the rock upon which we stand, the truth that empowers our words, and the promise that guides our actions. For in His sovereignty lies our greatest hope, our deepest comfort, and our most compelling call to action.

Humanity, Creation and Accountability

As we delve deeper into the concept of divine sovereignty, it becomes clear that every human being is intricately connected to a loving Creator. Our existence is not a mere coincidence or a product of chance; it is the result of an intentional act by God.

This realization has profound implications for our lives. It means that every person holds immense value and worth in the eyes of God. Each individual is handcrafted and uniquely designed by the Creator, imbued with purpose and potential.

But it also means that we are accountable to our Creator. Just as a potter has authority over their clay, God has authority over us as His creation. This accountability is not meant to be burdensome or oppressive; instead, it offers guidance and direction in living a fulfilling life.

In essence, knowing that we are created by God and accountable to Him can transform our perspective on life. It shifts the focus from ourselves to the One who holds us in His hands, from our own desires to the will of our Creator. And in doing so, it frees us from the superficial constraints of this world and invites us into a deeper relationship with God.

God's Divine Imprint on Humanity

In our quest to understand the complexities of life, the origin and purpose of humanity hold keys to unlocking profound truths about our existence. Central to this exploration is a truth that resonates through the ages, a truth grounded in the divine narrative of creation.

The Bible presents a clear and captivating account of our origin. It tells us, "So God created man in his own image, in the image of God created he him; male and female created he them" (Genesis 1:27). This passage beautifully illustrates that humanity was not the product of random chance or merely the next step in an evolutionary chain. Instead, we were meticulously crafted by God's almighty power, a special creation made to reflect His image.

This distinction is crucial, not only in theological discourse but in everyday living. It was upon this foundational truth that Christ built His teachings on marriage and familial relationships (Matthew 19:4), highlighting the intentional design and inherent value in every human being. When we grasp the fact that we are God's special creation, it enriches our understanding of our purpose and amplifies the importance of evangelism. God created us to enjoy a relationship with Him, to learn from Him, and to receive His blessings. Yet, sin has fractured this relationship, making personal salvation through Christ's sacrifice the only bridge back to God.

Understanding our creation by God carries with it a profound sense of responsibility. Contrary to the notion that we are masters of our fate, the Scripture reveals a different reality. We are not autonomous beings, free to live as we please without consequence. Our lives were intentionally designed by God, and as such, we are accountable to Him.

The Apostle Paul underscores this accountability when he declares,

"And the times of this ignorance God overlooked; but now commandeth all men everywhere to repent: because he hath appointed a day, in the which he will judge the world by that man whom he hath ordained" (Acts 17:30-31).

This pronouncement serves as a sobering reminder that a day of judgment is coming, one that has been ordained by God. Our actions, decisions, and very lives are subject to the divine scrutiny of a just and holy God.

What then, should be our response to these truths? Does the knowledge that we are created in the image of God, destined for fellowship with Him yet estranged by sin, stir your heart? It compels us to look beyond ourselves, to see the grandeur of God's plan for humanity, and to recognize the urgency of reconciliation through Jesus Christ.

Furthermore, it beckons us to live lives marked by purpose and accountability, knowing that we will one day stand before God. This realization prompts us to reevaluate our choices, to seek alignment with God's will, and to embrace the mission of sharing the hope of salvation with the world.

In reflecting on our divine origin and destiny, may we find renewed motivation to live out our calling with intentionality and grace, empowered by the knowledge that we are indeed fearfully and wonderfully made by God for a purpose far greater than we can imagine.

God Has Revealed Himself to Man

God has not remained a silent witness to man's plight. God has spoken to man. This is fundamental to all evangelism. Obviously if God has said nothing intelligible to man then man can hardly be expected to know what God expects of him and to do it.

The physical universe is a sermon from the Creator.

"The heavens declare the glory of God; and the firmament showeth his handywork" (Ps. 19:1).

No "dim light of nature" is this.

"For the invisible things of him from the creation of the world are clearly seen, being understood by the things that are made, even his eternal power and Godhead; so that they are without excuse" (Rom. 1:30).

The marvelous structure of the physical universe eloquently testifies to the genius and power of the God who made it.

The Word of God is also addressed to man though man in his blindness cannot grasp its message apart from divine illumination.

"All scripture is given by inspiration of God" (or, "God-breathed," II Tim. 3:16).

God has spoken in a world of mystifying beauty. He has also spoken in a Book of wondrous power—the Bible. Probably no more succinct description of evangelism in action could be given than that found in Acts 8:35:

"Then Philip opened his mouth, and began at the same scripture, and preached unto him Jesus."

Fruitful evangelism is inseparably connected with an inspired book containing the good news of God—the Bible.

God was not finished, however, in giving His message to men.

"God. . . hath in these last days spoken unto us by his Son" (Heb. 1:2).

God has written His love and His grace in the spotless life of the God-Man and upon the blood-stained cross at Calvary.

Salvation will never be secured through the pursuit of philosophy nor obedience to a man-made system. Man must know the true God as He has revealed Himself. Much modern philosophical and theological thought does not accept the fact the God has ever revealed Himself to man. For this reason the doctrine of personal salvation is obscured in most contemporary systems. If God has not spoken, or if it is doubtful as to what He has said, then obviously there is no authoritative answer for the burning question in the human soul: "What must I do to be saved?" (Acts 16:31).

From Desolation to Salvation

In the grand design of human experience, the reality of sin and salvation unfolds a deeply moving journey from despair to hope. The New Testament, especially Ephesians 2:1–7, provides deep insights into the human plight overshadowed by sin, highlighting the transformative power of God's grace.

The Apostle Paul does not mince words when he describes humanity's predicament. He states that individuals are "dead in trespasses and sins" (Ephesians 2:1). This stark declaration goes beyond suggesting that humanity is merely struggling or impaired by sin; it reveals a state of spiritual death—a complete and utter separation from the life found in God. Wrapped in the chains of our fleshly desires and disobedience, we find ourselves continually at odds with God and His Word, living in ways that displease the Lord (Ephesians 2:2).

This dire state leads to an unavoidable truth: without intervention, humanity is on a trajectory towards eternal separation from God, described vividly as being "children of wrath" (Ephesians 2:3). The immense truth of this separation evokes a sense of impending doom—a future marred by punishment and devoid of hope (Revelation 14:10-11).

The Lifeline of Divine Grace

Yet, in the midst of this bleak landscape, a beacon of hope emerges, illuminating the path to salvation. Ephesians 2:5 reveals the miraculous intervention of divine grace:

"Even when we were dead in sins, hath made us alive together with Christ, (by grace are ye saved)."

This passage underscores an essential truth—that salvation is not something we can achieve on our own. It is a gift from God (Ephesians 2:8), a testament to His boundless mercy and love for us because of the sacrifice of His Son, Jesus Christ.

What's even more remarkable is that the very faith required to grasp this lifeline of salvation is itself a manifestation of God's grace. We are not left to flounder in our efforts but are empowered by grace to believe and receive the promise of new life in Christ.

How, then, shall we respond to this profound revelation? Understanding our desperate need for forgiveness and grace and the magnificent gift of salvation offered through Christ invites us to reevaluate our lives. It challenges us to acknowledge our helplessness in sin and to receive the grace that brings life and hope.

The message of Ephesians 2 is not one of despair but a powerful reminder of the transformation possible through God's grace. It beckons us to move from a place of spiritual desolation to one of vibrant life in Christ, where we are no longer defined by our transgressions but by the limitless love and mercy of our Creator.

In this light, may we find the courage to confront the reality of our condition, to lay hold of the grace extended to us, and to step into the fullness of life that God has prepared for those who love Him. For in grace, we find the key to unlock our potential, live out our calling, and experience the true freedom that comes from being made alive in Christ.

Addressing The Doctrine of Election

In the midst of this grand design, we may wonder: who then is eligible for salvation? The answer lies in understanding that God's offer of grace and salvation is extended to all. In fact, John 3:16 proclaims that

"whosoever believeth in Him should not perish, but have everlasting life."

This invitation is inclusive—available to anyone who is willing to receive the gift of salvation through faith in Jesus Christ.

Yet, we must also recognize that while all are called, not everyone will respond to this call. The Bible tells us that some will reject the offer of grace and continue living in rebellion against God (Matthew 22:14). This rejection does not stem from any deficiency on God's part but from the stubbornness and unbelief of individuals, who choose to reject His love and mercy.

This concept is echoed in the parable of the wedding feast found in Matthew 22:1-14. In this story, a king invites guests to attend his son's wedding banquet but many refuse, even mistreating and killing those sent to invite them. The king then extends his invitation to all, but only those who come in the proper wedding attire are allowed to stay. This parable illustrates that while salvation is available to all, it requires a personal response and obedience to God's requirements.

The design of salvation is a remarkable journey from desolation to hope, made possible by God's amazing grace. It invites us to confront our spiritual condition, receive the gift of salvation through faith in Jesus Christ, and live a transformed life empowered by grace. This offer is extended to all, but only those who respond with faith and obedience are chosen to partake in the blessings of eternal life with God.

In light of the foregoing biblical illustration, in the grand narrative of faith, the process of evangelism is not a haphazard venture but a divinely orchestrated mission, deeply rooted in the intentional acts of the Trinity—God the Father choosing, God the Son redeeming, and God the Holy Spirit empowering. This profound partnership unveils the mystery and magnificence of salvation, presenting a tapestry woven with threads of divine purpose and grace.

The Sovereign Purpose and Saving Power

Ephesians 1 lays bare two monumental truths that anchor our understanding of salvation. First, there's the sovereign purpose denoted by "His will" (Eph. 1:5), illustrating God's preordained plan for humanity's redemption. This isn't a whimsical decision but a choice made from the infinite wisdom and pleasure of God, independent of human merit or actions, predicated solely on His benevolent desire.

Then, there's the saving power, encapsulated in the phrase "his grace" (Eph. 1:6), a testament to the unearned favor bestowed upon us. This grace isn't just a passive offering; it's an active, irresistible force that draws the chosen towards salvation, ensuring that the divine initiative reaches its intended completion. Scripture vividly portrays believers as "the called" (I Cor. 1:24), emphasizing that this calling is not a mere invitation but a compelling pull towards Christ, facilitated by the Holy Spirit.

Embracing the Mystery

The gospel holds within it a paradox that challenges human logic —the simultaneous existence of a universal invitation and a specific choice. While Ephesians speaks of predestination, 1 Timothy 2:1–7 reveals another dimension of God's heart—a fervent desire for all to encounter salvation. This duality might baffle our finite minds, yet it underscores the depth of God's love and the breadth of His mercy. He yearns for everyone to experience the fullness of His grace, providing a way through Jesus Christ, who "gave himself a ransom for all" (2:6).

It's natural to ponder how God's selection harmonizes with His open invitation to salvation. This mystery, while confounding, is not for us to unravel but to accept with humility, acknowledging that our understanding is limited. What remains clear, however, is the inclusive nature of God's call and the specificity of His choice, both rooted in a love so vast that it encompasses both the individual and the entirety of humanity.

Christ's sacrifice on the cross was a gift meant for all, an offering sufficient to cover every sin of every person across all time. Yet, this incredible act of love requires a response—a decision to accept or reject the grace extended. While Christ's atonement is universally sufficient, it becomes efficacious only when met with faith.

In this divine invitation to salvation, where grace leads and faith follows, we find our place. The knowledge that we are both individually chosen and collectively invited should inspire a response of gratitude, humility, and commitment. It beckons us to live in the light of this truth, sharing the hope of this great salvation, and extending the invitation to others so they too might find their way back to the heart of God.

In navigating the mysteries of faith, may we always lean into the assurance of God's sovereign love and the open invitation of His grace, empowering us to live out our calling with fervor and purpose.

Salvation Story

John Newton's conversion story is a powerful testament to the transformative power of God's grace and mercy. Once a captain of slave ships, Newton led a life marked by moral degradation and was deeply involved in the transatlantic slave trade. His path towards conversion began on a homeward voyage, when a violent storm battered his ship. Confronted with the imminent threat of death, Newton's heart was stirred towards repentance and prayer; he pleaded for God's mercy.

This moment of desperation sparked a gradual yet profound change in Newton's heart and life. Although he continued in the slave trade for a time after his conversion, he eventually became an ardent abolitionist, using his experiences and newly found faith to speak out against the horrors of slavery.

Newton's spiritual awakening led him to a deep and rich understanding of God's boundless grace—a theme that would forever mark his life and ministry. It was this understanding that inspired him to pen the words to one of the most beloved hymns of all time, "Amazing Grace." This hymn, which poignantly captures Newton's own transformation and redemption, has become an enduring symbol of hope and salvation for millions around the world.

The Integral Role of Every Believer in Evangelism

In the vibrant landscape of faith, every follower of Christ is called to share the message of salvation—a commission that transcends time, culture, and personal inclination. The narrative of Acts 8:4, where believers, not just church leaders, scattered and spread the word of God far and wide, serves as a compelling testament to our collective mission. This action wasn't limited to the apostolic circle but was a charge given to every disciple then—and by extension, to us today.

"Go ye into all the world and preach the gospel to every creature"
(Mark 16:15).

These words echo through the centuries, not merely as a directive but as an invitation to be part of something transcendent—the unveiling of divine grace to humanity. The early Christians, fueled by conviction, transformed their society from the inside out, bringing the message of hope to marketplaces, workshops, and homes. Their example challenges our contemporary understanding of evangelism, urging us to see it not as an isolated church activity but as a daily calling amidst our interactions to a world in need.

The Distinct Gift of Evangelism

While the mandate to evangelize is universal, Scripture reveals that the role of an "evangelist" carries a specific connotation. Figures like Philip, known as an evangelist (Acts 21:8), and Timothy, encouraged to "do the work of an evangelist" (II Tim. 4:5), exemplify this distinct ministry within the body of Christ (Eph. 4:11). The gift of evangelism—a divine enablement to effectively communicate the gospel—highlights that some believers are uniquely equipped to lead others to Christ.

This realization brings both clarity and comfort. Many faithful followers, despite earnest efforts, find that their personal witness does not always result in immediate conversions. This outcome can be disheartening, especially when faced with the misplaced notion that spiritual fervor alone guarantees widespread evangelistic success. Yet, Scripture offers reassurance; the kingdom of God flourishes on both sowing and reaping, recognizing that the impact of sharing one's faith extends beyond visible outcomes.

Understanding the gift of evangelism invites a broader appreciation for the diverse ways God uses His people in the mission field. It's essential to recognize that being a powerful voice for the gospel comes in many forms—some may plant seeds of faith with gentle conversations, while others may harvest souls through direct evangelistic outreach. Each role is pivotal, each effort valued in the eyes of God.

This perspective encourages believers who might not possess the gift of evangelism in its traditional sense but are nonetheless integral to the spread of the gospel. It also calls for a celebration of those endowed with this gift, acknowledging their critical role in leading lost souls to salvation.

A Collective Effort
Empowered by Individual Gifts

In the grand design of God's kingdom, each believer's contribution to evangelism, whether through daily witness or the specific calling of an evangelist, weaves together a rich tapestry of grace touching lives across generations. This understanding should empower us, inspire us, and unify us as we endeavor to live out the Great Commission.

Our mission field starts where our life happens—among friends, family, colleagues, and even strangers. May we, driven by love and guided by the Holy Spirit, seize every opportunity to share the life-transforming power of the gospel, honoring the unique ways God has equipped us to fulfill this sacred call.

From Conversion to Community

True evangelism, as depicted through the biblical lens, extends far beyond the initial moment of commitment—it's a pathway that leads from the joy of conversion to the depth of community life within the body of Christ. This spiritual voyage is not marked by fleeting encounters with faith but by enduring walks in the grace and knowledge of God in a healthy community of believers.

Consider the story of Lydia in Acts 16:14-15. Here, we witness the power of the gospel to open hearts and transform lives. Lydia, a businesswoman, not only embraced the message with her own heart but also saw her household come to faith, followed by their collective baptism. This wasn't merely an act of ritual; it was the outward expression of an inward revolution—a declaration of their new identity in Christ. Lydia's immediate shift from a new convert to a devoted supporter of Paul's ministry underscores the authentic change that genuine evangelism ignites.

Beyond Conversion to Community Integration

The essence of biblical evangelism doesn't rest on how many individuals pray the sinner's prayer, sign a conversion card, or participate in a baptismal ceremony, but rather on how these individuals grow and thrive within the community of faith long after their initial confession of faith. The early church in Philippi, likely including Lydia and her household, serves as a prime example. Their gatherings in Lydia's home (Acts 16:40), their communal worship, and their support for Paul's ministry reflect a vibrant, living faith that transcends individual belief to encompass a collective walk in truth.

Philippians 4:15-19 emphasizes the commendable support the Philippi church extended to missionary activities beyond their immediate sphere, highlighting the importance of contributing to missions outside one's own ministry. This church uniquely provided for church plants in Macedonia and Thessalonica, being the initial and sole supporter of these endeavors. As a result of their generosity,

God made a profound promise: "to supply all their needs according to His riches in glory by Christ Jesus" (Philippians 4:19), underscoring the reciprocal blessing of supporting God's work.

Paul's letter to the Philippians further highlights this, addressing not just individuals but a community united in faith, showcasing the New Testament model of evangelism—one that fosters spiritual growth and maturity within the church (Eph. 4:11–16).

The Ultimate Goal of Evangelism

The ultimate aim of evangelism, therefore, is not merely to increase the number of those confessing Christ but to cultivate disciples who, over months and years, demonstrate a steadfast commitment to living out their faith. They contribute to their congregations, engage in ministry, and lead their families in righteousness, embodying the transformation that comes from a true encounter with the gospel.

John encapsulates this beautifully when he writes, "I have no greater joy than to hear that my children walk in truth" (III Jn. 4). It's this ongoing walk—in truth, in grace, in community—that defines the success of evangelism. The New Testament calls us to a vision of evangelism that is as deep as it is wide, inviting believers not just to a moment of decision but to a lifetime of discipleship and growth within the body of Christ.

True evangelism, therefore, is a holistic process—a divine invitation to experience the fullness of life in Christ, from the moment of conversion, the waters of baptism, to the daily expressions of faith in a community that honors Him. It's a testament to God's desire for not just converts but disciples—individuals and families deeply rooted in the love and truth of Christ, growing together towards spiritual maturity. The command of Jesus was not to make converts but to make disciples.

In conclusion, the practice of evangelism is deeply intertwined with the study of theology. Evangelism, at its core, is an outworking of one's theological understanding of God, humanity, and salvation. It is theology in action—driven by the convictions that stem from a deep study of the things of God. The church that recognizes the symbiotic relationship between theology and evangelism positions itself for robust ministry and faithful witnessing. Theology informs our evangelistic efforts, providing the foundational truths on which our messages are built. Simultaneously, evangelism applies theology, turning doctrinal beliefs into living testimonies of faith.

Blessed indeed is the church that holds theology and evangelism in their proper perspective, understanding that one fuels and shapes the other. This acknowledgment not only enriches the church's witness but also deepens the believers' faith, ensuring that both the message proclaimed and the lives lived out are rooted in the truth of the Gospel. In navigating the path from conversion to discipleship, theology and evangelism must walk hand in hand, guiding the church in its sacred mission to make disciples of all nations.

Chapter 3

Born in Sin

Made Right Through Christ

Supernatural evangelism is an approach to spreading the message of Christianity that emphasizes the power of God and the supernatural in reaching others. It goes beyond traditional methods of evangelism, such as preaching and missionary work, by relying on divine intervention and spiritual gifts.

One of the key aspects of supernatural evangelism is the belief that God can work through believers to perform miracles, healings, and other supernatural acts to demonstrate his power and love to non-believers. This can include prophesying, casting out demons, or even raising the dead.

This approach to evangelism is rooted in biblical teachings, as Jesus himself performed many miracles and signs to draw people towards him and his message. In the book of Acts, we see how the early church continued this supernatural ministry, with the apostles and disciples performing miraculous acts in the name of Jesus.

However, it is important to note that supernatural evangelism does not rely solely on these extraordinary signs and wonders. It also involves building relationships and sharing one's personal testimony and the truth of the gospel in a loving and compassionate manner.

The goal of supernatural evangelism is not just to convert individuals, but also to bring about transformation and revival in communities and societies. By demonstrating the power of God through supernatural means, it can open hearts and minds to the truth of the gospel and lead people towards a deeper relationship with God.

While this approach may not be for everyone, it is a powerful tool that has been used throughout history to spread Christianity. It requires a strong faith and reliance on the Holy Spirit, but it can be incredibly effective in reaching those who may be resistant to traditional methods of evangelism.

Supernatural evangelism is an important aspect of sharing the message of Christianity. It allows us to tap into God's power and work alongside him in bringing others to know and experience his love and grace. As believers, it is our responsibility to share the good news of Jesus Christ in whatever way we can, and supernatural evangelism is just one powerful tool that we have at our disposal. So let us continue to pray for God's guidance and boldness as we seek to bring others closer to him through this approach.

As Paul says,

> *"And my speech and my preaching was not with enticing words of man's wisdom, but in demonstration of the Spirit and of power: That your faith should not stand in the wisdom of men, but in the power of God."* (1 Corinthians 2:4-5)

Successful, Supernatural Evangelism.

The Lord working with us. In the Great Commission given in Mark 16, the last verse states,

> *"And they went forth, and preached every where, the Lord working*
> *with them, and confirming the word with signs following. Amen."*
> (Mark 16:20)

This verse is a reminder that supernatural evangelism is not about our own abilities or eloquence, but rather about partnering with God and relying on his power and guidance.

The Interactive Work of the Holy Spirit. In 1 Corinthians 12:4-11, Paul explains the various spiritual gifts that are given to believers by the Holy Spirit. These gifts include prophecy, healing, and miracles - all of which can be utilized in supernatural evangelism. However, it is important to remember that these gifts are not for our own personal gain or glory, but for the building up of the church and the spreading of the gospel.

The Word of God. As mentioned earlier, supernatural evangelism is not just about powerful signs and wonders, but it also involves sharing the truth of the gospel through building relationships and personal testimony. And at the core of this message is the Word of God. It is through studying and understanding scripture that we can effectively share God's love and plan of salvation with others.

Prayer and Faith. In order for supernatural evangelism to be successful, it requires a strong foundation of prayer and faith. We must constantly pray for God's guidance and leading in our interactions with non-believers, as well as have the faith to step out in boldness and obedience when prompted by the Holy Spirit. As Jesus said in Matthew 17:20,

"If ye have faith as a grain of mustard seed, ye shall say unto this mountain, Remove hence to yonder place; and it shall remove; and nothing shall be impossible unto you."

With even the smallest amount of faith, we can see God's power working in miraculous ways.

Supernatural evangelism is not just a method or strategy, but a way of life for believers. It requires us to fully surrender ourselves to God and allow him to work through us in reaching others with the message of salvation.

Paul on Mars Hill

In Acts 17, we see an example of supernatural evangelism in action through the story of Paul on Mars Hill. When he arrived at Athens, Paul was greatly distressed by the city's many idols and began preaching in the synagogue and marketplace. However, his message caught the attention of some Greek philosophers who brought him to Mars Hill, a place where people gathered to discuss new ideas.

Paul used this opportunity to share the gospel with them, but he didn't just rely on his own words and reasoning. Instead, he allowed the Holy Spirit to guide him and used their own beliefs and experiences to bridge the gap between their understanding and the truth of God's word. He quoted scripture, referenced their poets and even used their altar to the "unknown god" as a starting point for his message.

Through his boldness, faith, and reliance on the Holy Spirit, Paul was able to effectively communicate the gospel and many people came to believe in Jesus. This is a powerful example of supernatural evangelism - using unconventional methods to reach people with the good news of salvation.

As believers navigating the currents of today's world, we stand in a position reminiscent of Paul's. Surrounded by individuals who may have a passing acquaintance with Christ but lack a deep, personal knowledge of Him and the profound truths of the Bible, we find ourselves amidst a sea of souls questing for meaning. They seek something beyond the visible, often searching in places that lead them further from the truth. In this era, spiritual emptiness has become a widespread affliction, with a tangible yearning for authentic, transformative truth.

How, then, can we, as believers, ignite a spark of genuine curiosity and understanding in a world drifting amidst confusion? How can we channel our lives, our businesses, and our ministries as beacons of hope and truth? The answer lies in our ability to live authentically, to integrate our faith seamlessly into every aspect of our lives, thereby communicating the gospel through our everyday lives. (2 Corinthians 3:1-3)

Through our actions, our words, and our unwavering commitment to our faith, we have the unique opportunity to be the light in the darkness, guiding others towards the profound truths that can change lives. Are we ready to rise to this challenge, to live out our faith boldly and unapologetically, and in doing so, inspire those around us to embark on a journey of discovery and transformation? The hunger for genuine, life-changing truth is palpable.

A Global Gospel

The call to share the good news of Christ transcends borders, reaching into every corner of the globe where missionaries serve. The challenge they, and we, face is monumental—a world ensconced in spiritual darkness, much like the one Paul faced on Mars Hill. But the answer remains unchanged. It is not merely about adopting new methods of evangelism or crafting more engaging stories. No, the solution lies in a divine empowerment, a supernatural strength that enables us to share the gospel with conviction and clarity.

For just as Paul demonstrated on Mars Hill, it is not our eloquence or strategies that will pierce the veil of indifference or disbelief. Instead, it is through the Spirit that our words find their mark, touching hearts and transforming lives. We are called to be vessels of this divine truth, empowered by a force greater than ourselves to bring light to the darkened corners of our world.

The Apostle Paul's Conversion Story (Acts 9)

The conversion of Saul, later known as the Apostle Paul, is one of the most profound and pivotal moments in the annals of Christian history. Saul, a rigid Pharisee and zealous persecutor of Christians, embarked on a mission to Damascus with the intent to arrest and bring to trial those following the Way of Jesus. However, his journey took an unexpected turn on the road to Damascus, marking the beginning of an extraordinary transformation.

As Saul neared Damascus, a blinding light from heaven suddenly engulfed him, casting him to the ground. From the brilliance emerged a voice,

> "Saul, Saul, why do you persecute me?" The bewildered Saul responded, "Who are you, Lord?"

The voice identified itself as Jesus, the one Saul was persecuting. Trembling and astonished, Saul was commanded to proceed into the city, where he would be told what he must do. The men traveling with Saul stood speechless, hearing the voice but seeing no one. Saul rose from the ground, his eyes open yet blinded by the light, depending on his companions to lead him by the hand into Damascus.

For three days, Saul remained blind and fasted, lost in contemplation and confusion. It was in this state that a disciple named Ananias was divinely instructed by God to visit Saul. Despite initial hesitation and fear because of Saul's notorious reputation, Ananias obeyed the vision, finding Saul on the Street called Straight. Laying hands on him, Ananias said,

"Brother Saul, the Lord Jesus, who appeared to you on the road as you came, has sent me so that you may receive your sight and be filled with the Holy Spirit."

Instantly, it was as if scales fell from Saul's eyes, and he could see again. He was then baptized, taking the first steps on a new path that would lead him to become one of Christianity's most fervent apostles.

Yet, the transformation of Saul was neither immediate nor simple. After his baptism, Saul spent three years with the local body of believers in Damascus, a critical period of learning, unlearning, and retraining. During these years, he was not idle but fervently prayed, studied the scriptures, and shared his testimony, all while receiving divine revelations that reshaped his understanding of the gospel. This period served as his preparation, a spiritual reformation that would equip him for the monumental task ahead. It was only after this time of growth and maturation in faith and doctrine that God would send him out to the nations, paving the way for Saul, now Paul, to spread the Christian faith across the world.

Paul's story, from a fierce persecutor to a foundational pillar of the Church, serves as a testament to the transformative power of the gospel and the boundless capacity for change within the human heart. His life illustrates the extraordinary lengths to which God will go to redeem a life, turning even the most unlikely individuals into instruments of His divine purpose.

In this mission, we are reminded of the words found in 2 Timothy 1:7,

"For God has not given us a spirit of fear, but of power and of love and of a sound mind."

This scripture underscores the essence of our calling—to move forward not in fear but in the power that comes from faith, armed with love and guided by wisdom. It encourages us to step out in faith, trusting that the same Spirit that empowered the former Saul, now Paul, on Mars Hill empowers us today.

The Components of the Gospel Message

At the core of the Gospel message, we explore a concept that resonates deeply with our understanding of the human condition and our profound need for redemption. This concept is often encapsulated in the term "Total Depravity," a theological notion that finds its roots in a pivotal passage from the New Testament, Romans 5:12. Here, we are confronted with a truth that has shaped the course of Christian thought:

"Wherefore, as by one man sin entered into the world, and death by sin; and so death passed upon all men, for that all have sinned."

Imagine a world untouched by sin. In such a world, the narrative of salvation would be unnecessary—no need for a Savior, no cross, no message of hope to spread across the nations. Yet, the introduction of sin through Adam's disobedience brought about a cataclysmic shift, marking the commencement of humanity's estrangement from divine perfection. This was not just a moment in history; it was the beginning of a story that affects every human being.

Why, then, is this understanding crucial for us today? Reflect on the impact of recognizing that, from the very start, our nature has been inclined away from God's original design. This realization brings into sharp focus the indispensable role of evangelism. It's not merely about sharing a set of beliefs but about extending an invitation to be part of a grand narrative of redemption and restoration.

Consider for a moment the gravity of what was lost through Adam's transgression. The consequences were far-reaching, affecting the spiritual and physical realms. Yet, in this acknowledgment lies the seed of hope—the very reason evangelism is not just important but essential. Through sharing the Gospel message, we offer a bridge back to reconciliation with God, a path that leads from death to life.

In light of this, we are called to action. How can we live out this calling in our daily lives, in our communities, and in our workplaces? The message of Romans 5:12 is not only a reflection on the past but a clarion call for the present and future. It compels us to recognize our role in God's redemptive plan, to see our lives as platforms for ministry, whether in business, relationships, or personal growth.

May we ponder deeply on our condition and the incredible opportunity before us to partake in the ministry of reconciliation. It's an invitation to step into our potential, to be agents of change in a world that yearns for hope and meaning. Thus, as we reflect on the significance of Total Depravity and its commencement, may we be inspired to take up the mantle of evangelism, empowered by the knowledge that through Christ, redemption is not just a possibility but a promise fulfilled.

Where it all Began

Adam's transgression stands as a pivotal event in the narrative of humanity, shaping the very foundation of our spiritual under-standing and moral accountability. The significance of Adam—and indeed, Eve—as historical figures cannot be overstated. Despite debates among scholars and theologians, some of whom regard the story of Adam as allegorical, their existence is crucial for the integrity of biblical teachings on sin and redemption.

The story of Adam is not merely a tale passed down through generations for its moral lessons; it represents a fundamental truth about human nature and our relationship with the divine. Romans 5:12 and subsequent passages underscore the reality of sin entering the world through the actions of two very real individuals, marking a moment of profound consequence for all of humanity. If we were to dismiss Adam as a fictional character, we would unravel the very fabric of Christian doctrine, leaving the principles of salvation and the need for a Savior in disarray.

Indeed, the historicity of Adam is not just a matter of theolog-ical debate but a cornerstone of faith that directly challenges modern narratives such as evolution. The biblical account asserts that humanity did not emerge through gradual processes from lesser beings but was created by God, endowed with moral respon-sibility from the outset. This understanding places us squarely before a holy God, accountable for our actions and in need of redemption—a stark contrast to the implications of an evolutionary origin devoid of divine creation and moral obligation.

Turning to the nature of Adam's sin, it was not an act committed in ignorance or deception. Unlike Eve, who was misled by the serpent's cunning, Adam chose to disobey God with full awareness of the repercussions. This decision, possibly motivated by his bond with Eve, introduced sin into the world in a manner that would affect every generation to follow. Scripture makes it clear, particularly through Paul's discussion in 1 Timothy 2:14, that while Eve was deceived, Adam's choice was deliberate—a distinction that underscores the gravity of his action.

Such deliberate disobedience brings to light the profound implications of Adam's sin. It wasn't merely an individual error but an act that severed the intended harmony between humanity and God, ushering in an era of spiritual estrangement and moral culpability for his descendants. This narrative isn't just a historical recount; it serves as a reminder of our collective fallibility and the enduring need for grace and salvation.

The profound impact of Adam's sin is captured in the pivotal declaration that *"sin entered into the world"* (Romans 5:12), marking a momentous shift in human history. This was not merely a singular act of disobedience; it was an event with ramifications that extended through all of humanity, embedding itself into the very fabric of our existence. The concept that *"death passed upon all men"* illustrates this pervasive spread of sin, indicating that its reach is universal, sparing no one from its influence. It's as though every aspect of human life, every relationship, and activity, has been touched by this initial transgression.

What makes Adam's sin so unique—and so devastating—is its dual nature. On one hand, it rendered every person a sinner, not just in practice but in essence, as if each one of us participated in that original act of rebellion. This might seem like a complex theological point, yet it's crucial for understanding how deeply intertwined we are with Adam's choice. The phrase often translated as *"all have sinned"* could be more accurately expressed as *"all sinned*," indicating a collective guilt that transcends time and individual actions.

This interpretation gains further clarity when considering the period from Adam to Moses, a time before God's law was formally codified. Despite the absence of a direct command to transgress against, death—the penalty for sin—reigned even over those who had never consciously violated God's statutes. This reality prompts a reevaluation of our understanding of sin and its consequences. It suggests that the repercussions of Adam's sin were not limited to him alone but were inherited by all humanity, regardless of personal deeds or knowledge of divine law.

Therefore, the sin of Adam goes beyond being a mere poor example for humanity to follow. It's not simply that he sinned and others imitated his disobedience. Rather, in a mystifying yet profound manner, all humanity sinned in and with Adam at that fateful moment. This shared guilt underlines the necessity of redemption and the profound grace offered through Christ, who represents a new possibility of liberation from this ancient burden. In light of this, we are invited to reflect deeply on our shared inheritance of sin and the equally shared offer of salvation, underscoring the critical role of faith and grace in our spiritual journey.

Therefore, revisiting the story of Adam and Eve compels us to reflect on our own spiritual journey and the universal quest for redemption. It reaffirms the necessity of evangelism—to share the hope of salvation through Christ with a world still grappling with the fallout from that fateful choice in the Garden of Eden. Through this lens, the account of Adam and Eve transcends time, urging us to confront our moral responsibilities and to seek, and preach, reconciliation with our Creator.

Born in Sin, Made Right Through Christ

Let's talk about why the story of Adam matters. The story of Adam and Eve in the book of Genesis is not just a piece of ancient mythology or a moral tale; it holds deep significance for our understanding of human nature and our relationship with God. The reality of Adam as a historical figure, along with his choice to disobey God, has far-reaching implications that continue to shape our lives today. As we delve deeper into the story of Adam, we are confronted with essential truths about sin, grace, and redemption, calling us to reflect on our collective need for salvation and the transformative power of Christ's sacrifice.

The historicity of Adam is not just a matter of theological debate but a foundational element in Christian doctrine. It serves as a critical link in the grand narrative of creation, fall, and redemption that underpins the entirety of Scripture. The New Testament writers assume Adam's existence and sin as historical fact, with Paul explicitly describing Adam as "the first man" (1 Corinthians 15:45). This understanding affirms our belief in a Creator God who intentionally designed humanity as moral beings, created in His image and with the capacity to choose between good and evil.

The significance of Adam's choice goes beyond personal responsibility; it extends to the fundamental state of humanity. Through this single act, sin entered into the world, radically altering our relationship with God and each other. The consequences were severe and pervasive, affecting every aspect of human existence—from our physical bodies to our moral conscience. This reality calls us to recognize the collective nature of sin and our shared inheritance of this fallen state, challenging any notion of self-righteousness or superiority.

However, as we confront the devastating effects of Adam's

disobedience, we are also reminded of God's grace and plan for redemption. In Christ, a new possibility is offered to humanity—a way out from under the weight of sin and death. Through His perfect obedience and sacrificial death on the cross, Jesus provides a path to forgiveness and reconciliation with God that was not possible before. This truth speaks to the universal human experience of sin and offers hope for restoration through faith in Christ.

The story of Adam is more than just a historical account; it holds profound theological significance for our understanding of human nature and God's plan for salvation. It reminds us of the universal reach of sin, inherited from our first parents, and the desperate need for a Savior. But it also reveals the vastness of God's love and grace, offering hope for redemption through faith in Christ. As we further reflect on this ancient story, may we be reminded of our shared need for salvation and our responsibility to share this good news with a world in desperate need of hope. The story of Adam and Eve is not just a tale of the past; it has deeply relevant implications for our present and future. It serves as a reminder of our human nature, both the potential for disobedience and the longing for redemption, which are universal experiences shared by all of humanity. This message resonates even more strongly in a world that is marred by sin and its devastating consequences.

The Why

The concept of "total depravity" paints a vivid picture of humanity's spiritual condition, deeply rooted in theological discourse and shaping our understanding of the need for divine grace. This term doesn't suggest that every individual acts in the worst possible manner or that people are inherently evil in their daily behaviors. Instead, it describes a state of spiritual estrangement from God—

where one's entire nature, will, and lifestyle are marred by sin, making it impossible to realign with God's desires without His intervention.

Why does this matter, especially when considering how we share the message of hope and redemption? The debate over humanity's spiritual state isn't just academic; it's a question that has sparked intense discussions and divided theologians throughout history. On one side was Pelagius, who believed in humanity's neutral moral standing, capable of choosing good or evil based on circumstances. Opposing him was Augustine, who argued for the inherent depravity and helplessness of man, unable to seek God without divine help.

This debate didn't end with them. James Arminius later introduced ideas that minimized God's sovereignty in favor of human choice, leading to a shift toward rationalism. Fast forward to the nineteenth century, Charles Finney, influenced by Arminian beliefs, argued against the notion of total depravity. He believed in the innate ability of individuals to turn towards God, emphasizing the human will over the Holy Spirit's transforming power.

These contrasting views raise fundamental questions about our approach to evangelism. If humanity is indeed in a state of total depravity, entirely incapable of seeking God without His grace, how does this shape our mission? Do we see the human will as completely ensnared by sin, or do we believe there's an inherent ability to choose the good?

Our perspective on these questions doesn't just influence theological debates but directly impacts how we engage with others about faith. If we lean towards the belief that people can be persuaded or motivated to choose faith through argument or influence, our evangelistic approach might focus on persuasion and rhetoric. But what does Scripture tell us about our fallen condition?

The Bible sheds light on these queries, portraying humanity's plight not as a mere moral failing but as a profound spiritual crisis that only divine grace can remedy. It encourages us to view evangelism not simply as a task of convincing minds but as a ministry of reaching hearts transformed by the Holy Spirit.

In this light, our conversations about faith become less about mustering arguments and more about sharing the hope and love that comes from God. Understanding the depths of our need for grace doesn't discourage us; rather, it underscores the beauty of redemption and the power of the Gospel to bring light into the darkest places. How, then, will we respond to this call to share the transforming love of Christ, knowing the deep need that exists in every human heart?

In the grand narrative of the Bible, the story of human fallibility begins with Adam and Eve, setting the stage for a theme of redemption that unfolds through the ages. This chapter has examined much of humanity's inherent sinful nature, traced back to our first parents, and the profound implications it holds for each of us today. Our discussion ventured through the theological debates surrounding total depravity, exploring how this concept shapes our understanding of human incapability to seek God without divine intervention.

However, the narrative does not end with despair. The beauty of the Christian faith emerges in the hope and redemption available through Jesus Christ. In Him, we find the answer to our fallen state, a divine remedy for our spiritual ailment. Christ's sacrifice on the cross stands as a monumental testament to God's love and grace, offering a way for us to be reconciled with Him, despite our sins.

This chapter aimed to bridge the ancient story with contemporary relevance, showing that our spiritual struggles are not isolated incidents but are part of a larger story of redemption. It calls us to a deeper understanding of our need for a Savior and the glorious hope we have in Christ. This realization is not meant to weigh us down but to lift our eyes to the One who can truly make us right with God.

As we move forward, may this knowledge inspire us to live with gratitude for the grace that frees us from the bonds of sin and compels us to share the message of hope with a world in need. Born in sin, we find our true identity and purpose not in our failings but in the redemptive work of Christ, made right through His love and sacrifice.

Chapter 4

The Utter Depravity of Sin

The concept of sin is a central tenet in the Christian faith. It refers to any thought, action, or attitude that goes against God's will and breaks his commandments. Sin is often described as the root cause of suffering, death and separation from God. But what exactly makes sin so utterly depraved? And how does it impact our everyday lives?

To answer these questions, we must first understand the nature of sin. Sin is not simply a mistake or a moral failing. It is a rebellion against God and his perfect will for our lives. This rebellion began with Adam and Eve's disobedience in the Garden of Eden and has been passed down to all humanity since then. This means that every person is born with a sinful nature and is prone to sinning.

But what makes sin so depraved is not just its origin, but its consequences. The Bible describes sin as bringing forth death - both physical and spiritual. Physical death refers to the end of our earthly life, while spiritual death refers to separation from God for eternity. This separation from God results in an eternity of suffering and separation from his love, mercy, and grace.

Sin also affects our everyday lives. It can lead to broken relationships, addictions, greed, and other harmful behaviors. It corrupts our thoughts and desires, causing us to put our own selfish desires above others'. Sin also hinders our relationship with God by creating a barrier between us and him. It prevents us from experiencing the fullness of his love, peace, and joy in our lives.

It's important to realize that sin was not a creation of God. Rather, humans were endowed with free will, granting them the choice to either follow God's commandments or rebel against them. In the Garden of Eden, Adam and Eve faced a pivotal choice: live in eternal paradise by obeying God, or defy Him by consuming the forbidden fruit from the Tree of the Knowledge of Good and Evil. Their choice to disobey marked the genesis of sin—a direct result of their own actions.

But there is hope. The Bible tells us that even though we are all sinners, God sent his son Jesus to die on the cross for our sins. Through his sacrifice, we can be forgiven and reconciled with God. By accepting Jesus as our Savior and turning away from our sinful ways, we can be made new and have eternal life with God. This does not mean that we will never sin again, but it means that we are no longer slaves to sin and can live a life of love, joy, and obedience to God.

In conclusion, the utter depravity of sin lies in its rebellion against God and its devastating consequences on our lives. But through Jesus, we have the opportunity to be freed from sin and experience a life filled with God's love, grace, and forgiveness. This is a powerful reminder of the magnitude of God's love for us and the importance of living a life aligned with his will.

Understanding Sin and Its Impact on Our Lives

As humans, we are all familiar with the concept of making mistakes or falling short of expectations. However, the Christian belief goes beyond simple moral failures and recognizes sin as a rebellion against God's perfect will for our lives. This rebellious nature is inherited from Adam and Eve's disobedience in the Garden of Eden, which has been passed down to all humanity. Let's explore the traits of sin and discover how we can liberate ourselves to live in the freedom that aligns with God's intentions.

Sin Represents Corruption

"But we are all as an unclean thing, and all our righteousnesses are as filthy rags . . ." (Is. 64:6).

Through this vivid imagery, the prophet Isaiah evokes the disturbing picture of a leper in the advanced stages of this dreaded disease, a condition that serves as a powerful metaphor for sin. Imagine the leper, some of his limbs missing, his eyes reduced to mere staring sockets, and his face marred beyond recognition. This stark image is what Isaiah uses to portray the depth of human sinfulness.

Under the laws of the Old Testament, lepers were required to live isolated from the community. They were considered unclean, and whenever others approached, they had to announce their impurity by shouting, "unclean." This not only signified their physical condition but also symbolized a deeper, spiritual estrangement and impurity.

The term "unclean" that Isaiah uses does not merely refer to the physical symptoms of leprosy but also to its accompanying odors and the societal perception of the disease. In a similar vein, sin can be seen as a kind of spiritual leprosy. It corrupts the soul, leaving it defiled and unrecognizable, much like the physical disfigurement caused by leprosy. Just as leprosy could render a person isolated and ostracized, sin separates individuals from the spiritual community and, ultimately, from divine connection.

The analogy of leprosy to sin serves as a stark reminder of the corrupting power of sin and its ability to disfigure the human soul, making it unrecognizable. It emphasizes the profound impact of sin on an individual's spiritual health and the necessity of seeking purification and redemption. Just as the leper in the Old Testament was seen as unclean and separated from the community, so too is the sinner marked by their transgressions, calling for a deep, transformative cleansing to restore their spiritual wellbeing.

Sin is Epitomized by Stubbornness

A compelling and vivid description of Israel's sinfulness is depicted in the sixth chapter of the Book of Jeremiah. Consider these poignant phrases: *"as a fountain . . . she casteth out her wickedness"* (Jer. 6:7) illustrating the continuous and unrepentant nature of their transgressions; *"their ear is uncircumcised . . . and . . . the word of the Lord is unto them a reproach"* (Jer. 6:10) indicating their deliberate refusal to listen or conform to divine guidance; *"every one dealeth falsely"* (Jer. 6:13) highlighting the pervasive dishonesty and deceit among them.

This outward rebellion and open refusal to obey God's commands reflect their deteriorated inner spiritual condition. Jeremiah conveys God's message, *"Thus saith the Lord, Stand ye in the ways and see, and ask for the old paths, where is the good way, and walk therein, and ye shall find rest for your souls."* Yet, they defiantly respond, *"We will not walk therein"* (Jer. 6:16) showcasing their obstinate refusal to return to the righteous path that promises peace and salvation.

Sin manifests profoundly in the obstinate refusal of the godless to heed the Lord's warnings and accept His gracious invitations. Their adamant declaration, "We will not," mirrors a deep-seated rebellion. Despite God's offers of salvation, eternal life, and the promise of profound peace to those willing to accept it, their response remains a stubborn "we will not." Sinners, in this regard, exhibit a hard and impenitent heart (Rom. 2:5), a condition characterized by unyielding stubbornness. Their hearts, hardened against the Lord, are impervious to his call and resistant to His mercy and grace. This narrative not only sheds light on the nature of sin but also serves as a cautionary tale about the dangers of stubbornness and the refusal to seek redemption and transformation through God's love.

Sin Leads to Spiritual Blindness

The condition of the unsaved is marked by an inability to understand or appreciate spiritual truth. Their understanding is darkened, as described in Ephesians 4:18, leaving them in a state of spiritual blindness. This blindness prevents them from grasping the essence of spiritual realities and truths. Without the intervention of divine grace, a lost person remains unable to comprehend the concept of the new birth, echoing the confusion of Nicodemus when he asked, *"How can these things be?"* as recorded in John 3:9. This spiritual blindness is not accidental but is the direct result of Satan's work. He has *"blinded the minds of them which believe not,"* as stated in II Corinthians 4:4, to keep them from seeing the illuminating light of the Gospel.

The predicament of the unsaved is such that no amount of human reasoning or persuasive argument can pierce through the darkness that envelops their understanding. They are completely impervious to our most well-crafted arguments and logical presentations of spiritual truth. The veil that covers their minds and hearts must be lifted, and the deep darkness that surrounds them must be penetrated. However, this is a task that no human effort can achieve on its own. It necessitates a supernatural intervention.

This divine intervention comes through the work of the Holy Spirit, who alone has the power to bring sight to their blinded minds. It is through His sovereign and gracious actions that the veil is removed and the light of the Gospel shines forth into their hearts. The Holy Spirit uses the Word of God as His tool, making it alive and active in the hearts of the unsaved. As the Scriptures are proclaimed and shared, the Holy Spirit works to illuminate minds, convict hearts, and draw individuals to the truth of God's saving grace. Through this powerful work, those who were once blind are now able to see, and the beauty of the Gospel becomes a glorious reality to them.

Sin Makes You Powerlessness

The concept of sin plunges human beings into a state of absolute helplessness, a condition where one is "fast bound in sin and nature's night," as eloquently described by the hymn writer. This portrayal highlights the profound depths of human incapacity to escape from the grip of sin without divine intervention.

Jesus Christ Himself illuminated this condition with stark clarity, saying,

> "No man can come to me, except the Father which hath sent me draw him: and I will raise him up at the last day" (John 6:44).

This statement is not just a casual remark; it is a potent declaration of the human state in relation to divine grace. Christ emphasized that the journey towards God is not merely a matter of human decision or effort. Instead, it necessitates a "drawing," an irresistible pull, a supernatural moving of God's Holy Spirit upon a person's heart. This divine action is the only remedy for sin, which has completely disabled mankind, rendering them incapable of seeking God through their own volition or strength.

The concept that sin has not just marred but completely disabled man, extends beyond the simple act of persuading an individual to "make a decision" for God. It involves liberating the mind and heart from the shackles that tightly bind them, a task only achievable through divine power. This notion is supported by historical doctrinal statements articulated by English Baptists. In their profound examination of sin, they declared,

> "From this original corruption, whereby we are utterly indisposed, disabled, and made opposite to all good, and wholly inclined to all evil, do proceed all actual transgressions."*

This confession eloquently captures the essence of human helplessness under sin, emphasizing that from the corrupted state of humanity, all forms of transgressions emerge. It underscores the belief that every act of sin finds its roots in the innate corruption that sin has implanted in the human heart, a corruption so deep and pervasive that it tilts the human inclination wholly towards evil and away from all that is good.

Therefore, the sinner's condition is one of utter helplessness, trapped in the darkness of sin and unable to break free without the transformative grace of God. It is a state that necessitates not just a superficial acknowledgement but a profound, divine intervention

---

* London Confession of 1677

to restore the sinner to a state of grace and enable them to embrace the path towards righteousness. This understanding serves as a cornerstone of the faith, reminding believers of the profound need for God's grace and the power of the Holy Spirit to initiate and sustain a life transformed from sin to salvation.

Sin Leads to Spiritual Death

What exactly is the spiritual condition of someone who sins? Paul provides a stark assessment in his letter to the Ephesians, stating that the individual is "dead in trespasses and sins" (Ephesians 2:1). This description paints a vivid picture of the sinner's state; he possesses absolutely no spiritual vitality. It's crucial to understand that the sinner is not simply unwell or impaired in a minor way—they are entirely devoid of life in a spiritual sense. This realization is not just a theological nuance; it holds profound implications for our approach to evangelism. Recognizing that we are dealing with individuals who are spiritually dead, not just weak or misguided, underscores the urgency and necessity of our mission to bring the message of salvation and life.

The Utter Depravity of Sin

The implications of the doctrine of total depravity stretch far beyond individual salvation. It affects our understanding of human nature, society, and even the world at large. Total depravity teaches that all aspects of humanity are corrupted by sin and that there is nothing inherently good within us. This notion stands in stark contrast to other philosophies and belief systems that proclaim the inherent goodness or potential of humanity.

However, the teachings of total depravity emphasize that without the transformative power of God's grace, there is no hope for true righteousness or goodness in our lives. It also highlights the need for constant dependence on God and His Spirit to overcome the corrupting effects of sin in our daily lives.

In addition, the doctrine of total depravity reminds us that our fight against sin is not just an individual struggle, but a collective one. We are all affected by sin and its consequences, and it takes the grace of God working within us to overcome its destructive effects. This understanding calls for unity and compassion towards our fellow human beings, recognizing that we are all in need of salvation and redemption through Christ.

As believers, it is vital to hold on to the doctrine of total depravity, not as a means to condemn or judge others, but as a reminder of our need for God's transforming grace in our lives. It should also compel us to share the message of salvation with those who are still trapped in sin's deadly grip, that they too may be drawn by God's powerful and saving grace towards true life in Him. So, the doctrine of total depravity not only highlights our helpless condition but also serves as a reminder of the immeasurable love and redeeming power of God through Christ. By understanding this doctrine, we can better comprehend the depths of our need for salvation and appreciate the magnitude of God's grace that enables us to overcome sin and embrace righteousness.

God Draws the Sinners Heart to Repentance

Having established the complete helplessness of the sinner, it is essential to note that human efforts alone are futile in bringing about true repentance and transformation. No amount of human wisdom, persuasion, or motivational speeches can fully convince an individual to turn away from their sinful ways and embrace God's grace. As Christ Himself stated in John 6:44, "No one can come to Me unless the Father who sent Me draws him," highlighting the necessity of divine intervention in salvation.

The sinner is entirely impervious to human power and persuasion, blinded by sin's deception and enslaved by its powerful grip. The only remedy for this spiritual blindness and bondage is through the grace of God, initiated by His love towards us and made possible through Christ's sacrifice on the cross. This understanding should humble us and remind us that our role is to share the message of salvation, but ultimately it is God who draws hearts towards Him.

The Conversion Story of Andrew Klavan

Andrew Klavan's journey to faith stands as a profound testament to the power of grace over the totality of human depravity and the limitations of mere human effort in achieving true conversion. Klavan, a renowned author and commentator, spent much of his adult life as a secular Jew, deeply skeptical of Christianity and any form of religious faith. His path towards Christianity was neither quick nor straightforward, marked by intellectual curiosity, profound personal struggles, and a relentless quest for truth.

Klavan's conversion story began in earnest during a period of personal turmoil and existential questioning. Despite his success as an author, he grappled with a deep-seated sense of unhappiness and a pervasive feeling that something was missing from his life. This existential crisis propelled him on a quest for truth, leading him to explore various philosophical and religious traditions in search of answers.

The turning point came unexpectedly through the arts, a domain where Klavan had always felt at home. It was the beauty, complexity, and depth of Christian-themed works of art and literature that first opened his heart to the possibility of the divine.

These encounters with beauty acted as silent whispers of God's existence and love, challenging his skepticism and drawing him towards the Christian faith.

However, intellectual assent to Christianity's claims was only part of Klavan's journey. The full realization of his need for God's grace came through personal experiences that highlighted his own sinfulness and the profound emptiness of a life lived without God. It was through reading the Bible, prayer, and the influence of Christian friends and writers that Klavan eventually came to acknowledge Jesus Christ as his Savior and Lord.

Klavan's conversion is a powerful illustration of how God's grace can penetrate the most resistant of hearts, transforming skepticism and unbelief into faith and devotion. His story underscores the essential truth that our efforts alone cannot lead to salvation; it is only through the drawing power of God, manifested in diverse and often unexpected ways, that true conversion takes place. Andrew Klavan's testimony serves as a beacon of hope for all who seek truth and demonstrates the boundless nature of God's grace that can reach even those who seem farthest away.

The Urgency of the Gospel Message

Hell is not an allegory or a figment of our imagination, its a real place! The doctrine of total depravity should serve as a sobering reminder of the consequences of sin and the urgent need for salvation. Without Christ's sacrifice and God's grace, every human being is eternally lost, condemned to suffer in hell.

This reality should compel us as believers to share the gospel message with urgency and compassion. It should move us to pray fervently for the lost and to actively seek opportunities to share the hope of salvation with those who are yet to experience God's transforming grace. Time is short, and eternity is at stake for every soul.

At the same time, we must also remember that our role is not one of judgment or condemnation but of love and reconciliation. We are called to be ambassadors of Christ, sharing His message of love and redemption with a world lost in sin. The doctrine of total depravity should lead us to approach others with humility, compassion, and the understanding that we too were once dead in our sins but now have been made alive through God's grace.

The doctrine of total depravity is not one that should cause fear or guilt, but rather it should point us to the immeasurable love and grace of God that saves us from our helpless condition. It should also remind us of the urgency and importance of sharing this message with a world in desperate need of salvation. May we never lose sight of the depth of our need for God's grace and may it move us to share His love with others, knowing that it is only through His drawing power that hearts can be truly transformed.

The Conversion Story of C.S. Lewis

C.S. Lewis, a towering figure in literature and Christian apologetics, underwent a remarkable transformation from staunch atheism to becoming one of the most influential Christian writers of the twentieth century. His conversion story is a compelling narrative of intellectual and spiritual evolution, marked by rigorous skepticism and the relentless pursuit of truth.

Lewis's early life was steeped in religious ambivalence; his youthful Christian faith was eroded by the death of his mother when he was just nine, leading to a period of atheism grounded in a materialist worldview. He pursued a rigorous study of classics, philosophy, and literature at Oxford University, where the seeds of doubt began to sprout regarding his atheistic convictions.

His journey from atheism back to Christianity was gradual and complex, deeply intertwined with his academic and literary pursuits. Lewis often credited his friends and colleagues, including J.R.R. Tolkien and Hugo Dyson, as significant influences in his conversion process. Through prolonged discussions and debates, particularly with Tolkien, Lewis came to appreciate the Christian narrative not only as a myth but as the true myth that intersected with history and reality in the person of Jesus Christ.

The pivotal moment for Lewis came in 1931, after a long conversation with Tolkien and Dyson on the truth of Christian myths and their fulfillment in Christ. Following this discussion, Lewis noted in his autobiography, *Surprised by Joy*, that he converted to theism on a motorcycle ride to the zoo with his brother, saying, "When we set out, I did not believe that Jesus Christ is the Son of God, and when we reached the zoo, I did." His conversion to Christianity itself would follow on later, culminating in his acceptance of Jesus Christ as not merely a mythic hero, but as the living Son of God who died and rose again for the salvation of humanity.

Lewis's conversion was not marked by overwhelming emotional experiences but was a rational and imaginative assent to the claims of Christianity. It led to a profound shift in his writings, from his early works characterized by skepticism to books that vigorously defended the Christian faith, such as *Mere Christianity*, *The Problem of Pain*, and *Miracles*. Furthermore, his fiction, notably *The Chronicles of Narnia*, subtly reflects his Christian worldview, aiming to kindle a sense of divine wonder and truth among his readers.

C.S. Lewis's conversion underscores the importance of intellectual engagement with faith, the role of friendship and conversation in spiritual journeys, and the capacity of Christianity to provide a coherent and compelling framework for understanding the world. His story serves as an inspiration for those wrestling with doubts and searching for truth, reminding us that the path to faith often winds through the terrains of reason, imagination, and community.

The Path to Liberation from Sin

In conclusion, the gravity of sin's impact on the human condition cannot be overstated. It entraps individuals in a cycle of spiritual blindness, absolute helplessness, and ultimately leads to spiritual death. The Scriptures have made it abundantly clear that there is no human deed or merit that can suffice to break these chains—redemption and restoration come solely through divine grace and intervention. It is only through acknowledging our utter incapacity to liberate ourselves from sin's grasp and turning to God in repentance and faith that we can hope to be set free.

The role of the Holy Spirit is pivotal in this process of liberation. Through His convicting power, individuals are brought to a profound awareness of their sinfulness and need for a Savior. It is He who works in the hearts, softening and preparing them to receive the truth of the Gospel. The message of Jesus Christ's atoning sacrifice on the cross is the beacon of hope for all humanity. It is by placing our faith in Him and His redemptive work that the chains of sin are broken, and we are granted the gift of eternal life.

Our response to this life-changing truth must be one of humble submission and trust in God's gracious provision for our salvation. The act of turning from sin and entrusting oneself to Christ is the beginning of a transformational journey. Through His grace, we are not only set free from the penalty of sin but are also empowered to live lives that reflect His righteousness. The pathway out of the darkness of sin and into the light of Christ's love is open to all who will receive Him by faith.

As believers, we are called to share this message of hope and freedom with a world ensnared by sin. Understanding the depth of sin's impact on the human soul reinforces the urgency of our mission to proclaim the Gospel. It is in Christ alone that the captives can be set free, and lives can be transformed. Therefore, as ambassadors for Christ, we must seek to reach out to the lost with compassion, clarity, and the life-giving message of the Gospel, inviting them to experience the liberating power of God's grace and love.

Chapter 5

Victorious Evangelism

I n the heart of the message that has echoed through time, a message of profound love and grace, lies the foundation of our faith—the gospel. This good news, which pulsates with the victory over sin secured by a vicarious Substitute, is what we call the *"gospel of God"* (cf. 1 Timothy 1:11). It's a testament to the eternal love of God, the Great Evangelist, whose divine strategy for salvation illuminates our path with the light of His marvelous grace.

Yet, as we stand today, we find ourselves amidst a concerning panorama. Christ's unequivocal directive to spread the gospel across the globe starkly contrasts with a noticeable indifference among many believers towards this call. Sandwiched between this divine mandate and our collective inertia are countless souls strewn across the world—many of whom traverse life's journey without once hearing the name of Jesus. The reality is stark: a vast expanse of humanity remains ensnared in spiritual obscurity, with entire nations under the grip of false doctrines. Amidst this, the community of true believers, those reborn in spirit, seems but a mere whisper in the cacophony of the world's populace.

Despite the fervent efforts of missionaries and the heartfelt appeals made, the ratio of gospel-bearers to the global population is dishearteningly disproportionate. From a human viewpoint, the endeavor of evangelism might seem teetering on the brink of failure—a monumental task seemingly insurmountable.

However, herein lies a pivotal truth: if the fulfillment of Christian evangelism were to rest solely on human capabilities, it would indeed be doomed to falter. Humanity, with all its limitations, imperfections, and frailties—even at its zenith of dedication—remains fundamentally flawed. The most devoted among us, those who tirelessly sow the seeds of faith, are often the first to acknowledge their shortcomings, their distance from the ideal they strive towards.

But, let us not forget, brothers and sisters, that our strength lies not in our might but in His. Scripture reminds us,

"Not by might, nor by power, but by my Spirit, says the Lord of hosts" (Zechariah 4:6).

The essence of our mission, the very core of our calling, transcends the boundaries of human effort and capability. It is a divine assignment, a commission, empowered and sustained by the Spirit of God. This is our calling. This is our mission. To venture forth, armed with faith and love, into the heart of darkness, bearing the torch of the gospel—not by our strength but by His. Together, as a united body of believers, empowered by the Spirit, we can transcend the barriers of apathy and limitation. We can be the vessels through which His light shines forth, bringing hope, faith, and transformation.

Partners Together With God

In a world that often seems divided between the divine and the mundane, a harmonious approach to evangelism emerges from the New Testament, offering a path that intertwines our earthly endeavors with our spiritual duties. Evangelism, the act of sharing the good news, is not just a calling but a responsibility entrusted to the born-again children of God. It beckons us to ponder,

"How shall they hear without someone preaching to them?"
(Romans 10:14).

This rhetorical question underscores the pivotal role we play in the divine narrative, highlighting the privilege we have been given to be partners together with God in this sacred mission.

Yet, as we venture forth on this path, it's crucial to recognize that the ultimate success of God's plan for evangelism doesn't solely hinge on our efforts. We, in our human frailty, might stumble and falter, but the divine strategy is flawless and unfailing. God, in His omnipotence, ensures that His purpose is fulfilled. This truth offers both comfort and a challenge. While it reassures us that God's plan is invincible, it also reminds us of the accountability we share in this grand design.

God's method of correcting and guiding us through His Word, and the teachings of faithful preachers and teachers, serves as both a rebuke for our failures and a beacon guiding our way. At the judgment seat of Christ, our actions and inactions in this Great Commission will be scrutinized.

Therefore, as we align our professional lives with our spiritual calling, we are invited to unlock our potential and live out our calling with an empowered spirit. We are called not just to be bystanders but active participants in God's evangelistic purpose. Our mission transcends mere personal business; it's a ministry woven into the very fabric of our daily lives.

The Salvation Story of
William and Catherine Booth

The Salvation Story of William and Catherine Booth, Founders of the Salvation Army, epitomizes the power of faith translated into action. William Booth, born in 1829, began his evangelistic pursuits in the mid-1800s, initially as a Methodist preacher. It was during this period of fervent evangelism that he met Catherine Mumford, whose commitment to social reform and theological congruity matched his own. Together, they embarked on a mission that would not only challenge the conventions of their time but also lay the foundation for a global movement devoted to the spiritual and physical salvation of the downtrodden.

In 1865, the Booths established The Christian Mission in the East End of London, a decrepit area marred by poverty, homelessness, and vice. This mission marked the inception of what would later become the Salvation Army. The Booths' innovative approach to ministry, characterized by open-air meetings, the use of brass bands to attract crowds, and an unwavering focus on the redemption and rehabilitation of society's most marginalized, was revolutionary.

Their strategy, while initially met with skepticism and even hostility, eventually garnered widespread acclaim for its effectiveness in outreach and social reform. The Salvation Army's emphasis on practical Christianity—feeding the hungry, sheltering the homeless, and advocating for social change—stemmed directly from the Booths' theological understanding that faith must manifest in works of love and justice. Their legacy, upheld by the worldwide influence of the Salvation Army, stands as a powerful testament to their steadfast belief that the gospel offers not just a path to spiritual salvation, but also an opportunity to showcase the positive outcomes of partnering with God.

Victorious Evangelism Began in the Heart of God

Ultimately, the victory of Christian evangelism began in the heart of God. It was His plan to reconcile humanity with Himself and restore creation to its intended purpose. In the fullness of time, He sent His Son, Jesus Christ, as the ultimate sacrifice for our redemption. Through His death and resurrection, we have been given new life, equipped and empowered by the Holy Spirit to continue His work on earth.

The Mystery Behind the Origin of Sin

The enigma surrounding the origin of sin presents a deeply complex puzzle. How could an all-powerful, supremely good God be linked to the emergence of sin? This question has not only perplexed theologians for centuries but has also led to a wealth of scholarly discourse aimed at understanding how the existence of evil can coexist with the concept of a benevolent Creator who reigns with absolute sovereignty. The intricacies of this debate are vast, touching upon various doctrines and theological perspectives. Yet, amidst these discussions, a significant agreement surfaces among many conservative theologians and devout believers: the clear exoneration of God from being the progenitor of sin.

How is this possible? While it's clear that God did not create sin, it's equally understood that humans were given free will, allowing them the option to either adhere to God's commandments or to defy them. In the Garden of Eden, Adam and Eve stood at a crossroads: to live in everlasting paradise by adhering to God's commandments, or to challenge His authority by partaking of the forbidden fruit from the Tree of Knowledge of Good and Evil. Their choice to disobey marked the genesis of sin—a direct result of their own actions. Consequently, sin was not a creation of God, but rather a result of human disobedience.

However, the narrative takes a fascinating turn when considering the role of sin within the grand tapestry of divine providence. Scripture reveals a profound truth – the presence of sin, while perplexing, is intricately woven into God's eternal plan. This acknowledgment does not serve to besmirch the character of God or to question His omnipotence. On the contrary, it serves to underscore His unfathomable sovereignty and the meticulous execution of His will throughout the annals of history.

In this vein, the words of John in the context of end-time prophecy shed light on this profound mystery. Revelation 13:8 offers a glimpse into the divine foreknowledge and the preordained solution to the problem of sin, stating,

> "And all that dwell upon the earth shall worship him, whose names are not written in the book of life of the Lamb slain from the foundation of the world."

This scripture, while open to interpretation, strikes at the heart of a profound theological truth: the provision for humanity's salvation through the sacrifice of Jesus Christ, the Lamb, was established before the creation of the world. This premeditation suggests that the eventuality of sin, and consequently the need for redemption, was foreseen by God and integrated into His eternal design.

Such a perspective does not trivialize sin or its consequences but rather highlights the depth of God's redemptive plan and His supreme authority over all of creation. It underscores the complexity of God's relationship with time, His foreknowledge of human actions without infringing on free will, and the ultimate demonstration of His love through the provision for salvation. Thus, while the question of sin's origin and its allowance in God's creation remains a challenging theological puzzle, the acknowledgment of sin's role within God's overarching plan invites believers to delve deeper into the mysteries of faith, sovereignty, and divine grace.

Divine Provision Through Christ

The scripture further solidifies this truth, affirming that the crucifixion of Christ was not a mere historical event but a preordained fulfillment of God's salvation plan. Acts 2:23 attests to this, stating that Christ was

"handed over by God's deliberate plan and foreknowledge".

The Cross of Calvary stands as a testament to God's unfathomable wisdom and His unyielding commitment to redeem humanity. In His infinite love, God ordained a way of salvation for all willing to embrace it, offering redemption through the sacrifice of His own Son, who bore the weight of sin's penalty.

This narrative of victorious evangelism, beginning in the heart of God, invites us into a deeper reflection on our role within God's grand scheme. It challenges us to contemplate the magnitude of God's foresight and the depths of His grace. By understanding that our redemption was etched into the framework of eternity, we are called to live lives that reflect this marvelous truth, bearing witness to the light of salvation that shone forth from the foundation of the world.

In this divine orchestration, we find not only the answer to the enigma of sin but also the assurance of our place within God's eternal narrative. It beckons us to engage in a life of ministry and service, empowered by the knowledge that we participate in a victory already secured, a plan divinely ordained, and a love that transcends time itself.

Victorious Evangelism Moves through the Hearts of Believers

Therefore, as believers, we are called to embrace our role as ambassadors of God's redemptive plan. Through victorious evangelism, we carry forth the message of salvation and share in the joy of seeing lives transformed by God's grace. Our hearts should be moved with compassion for those who have not yet experienced the life-changing power of Christ's sacrifice.

Within the context of the book of Acts both the sovereign grace of God and fervent evangelistic and missionary effort are set forth. Paul in his missionary travels came to Antioch. He preached Christ there. The inspired historian described what happened.

> *"And when the Gentiles heard this, they were glad, and glorified the word of the Lord: and as many as were ordained to eternal life believed"* (Acts 13:38).

Here the power of the gospel is the cause of the successful evangelism described. There was no one evangelical method employed by Paul. His preaching and manner in each place varied as the occasion demanded.

Born Again

In Thessalonica, he preached three sabbath days reasoning with people out of the scriptures (Acts 17:2). In Athens, he contended in synagogues & marketplaces during an open-air discourse on Mars Hill to Athenian philosophers (Acts 17:16-34).Paul encountered opposition but adhered to his evangelistic mission. In a legal setting, he gave his testimony to Roman authorities in Caesarea (Acts 25:23). Regardless of the circumstances, Paul was steadfast in sharing the gospel and bringing others into the fold of salvation.

God Works Through Obedient Believers

Through these accounts, we see that God works through the obedience and faithful witness of believers to bring about His purposes. The book of Acts is a testament to this truth, as it showcases how the early church grew and spread through the dedicated efforts of believers who shared the gospel in word and deed.

Evangelist T.L. Osborne in India

In the annals of modern evangelism, T.L. Osborn's crusades stand as towering beacons of God's work through an obedient servant. Among the many stories of miraculous conversions and healings, one event in particular encapsulates the profound impact of Osborn's ministry. In the mid-20th century, during a crusade in India, a nation marked by its rich tapestry of religions and languages, Osborn preached the Gospel with his characteristic fervor and faith. Amidst the multitude, a man crippled from birth was brought forward. Having lived a life confined by his disabilities, the man held little hope, yet something extraordinary happened that day.

81

As T.L. Osborn shared the message of Jesus Christ's love and salvation, faith ignited in the hearts of the listeners. In a moment that would mark a turning point for thousands witnessing, Osborn prayed for the crippled man in the name of Jesus. Miraculously, the man began to move, stand, and eventually walk for the first time in his life. The crowd was awestruck, and this act of divine intervention pierced the hearts of many, leading to an unprecedented number of conversions.

This event not only showcased the miraculous power of God but also exemplified the core of Osborn's evangelistic mission - to demonstrate God's love and power in tangible, life-changing ways. It served as a catalyst for further evangelistic endeavors in India and beyond, leaving an indelible mark on the history of Christian missions. Through T.L. Osborn's faithfulness and the work of the Holy Spirit, the Gospel was preached, lives were transformed, and the message of Christ's redemptive love spread across nations.

The Miraculous Ministry of
Reinhard Bonnke in Africa

In the lineage of great evangelists who operated under the banner of faith and miracles, Reinhard Bonnke stands out, particularly for his unwavering commitment to spreading the Gospel across the continent of Africa. His ministry was marked by countless instances of divine intervention, but one testimony vividly encapsulates the supernatural impact of his obedience to God's calling.

During one of Bonnke's tent meetings in Nigeria, an extraordinary occurrence demonstrated the power of God at work through his ministry. A man, who had been declared dead for three days and was being transported in a van to his final resting place, was brought to the meeting by relatives who harbored the faintest hope for a miracle. Amidst the gathering of thousands, as prayers ascended and faith permeated the atmosphere, something miraculous unfolded. Bonnke, moved with compassion and guided by the Holy Spirit, prayed for the deceased man. In moments that followed, to the astonishment of everyone present, the man began to stir. Gradually, he regained consciousness, and eventually, fully revived, stood up, testifying to the life-giving power of Jesus Christ.

This miraculous event became a defining moment in Bonnke's ministry, illustrating not only his deep faith in the Gospel's power but also the profound ripple effect of obedience to God's call. The news of this resurrection miracle spread like wildfire, significantly bolstering the faith of believers and drawing countless others to seek the truth of the Christian message.

Reinhard Bonnke's life and ministry were a testimony to the fact that when believers step out in obedience to God's calling, heaven moves, and the earth witnesses the undeniable power of the Gospel. Through his ministry, millions were reached, and the landscape of Christianity in Africa was forever altered, showcasing the enduring legacy of evangelistic ministry grounded in faith, obedience, and the miraculous.

God Works Through the Preaching of His Word

Make no mistake about it. Evangelism is more than visible miracles, it also includes powerful gospel preaching and personal witnessing. Men are not saved in a vacuum. They are saved as they hear God's Word delivered through dedicated servants.

Perhaps we may recoil at the statement that they were "ordained to eternal life" and thus "believed" (Acts 13:48). Do not forget, however, that this statement is immersed within a context of preaching. At least seven verses in this chapter indicate or declare, directly or indirectly, that God's Word was preached:

1. Acts 13:5 - *"they preached the word"*
2. Acts 13:7 - *"he gave him the charge saying, 'preach'"*
3. Acts 13:14 - *"Paul stood up and beckoning with his hand said, 'men of Israel . . . hear my words'"*
4. Acts 13:42 - *"As Paul and Barnabas went out . . . they persuaded them to continue in the grace of God. And the next Sabbath day came almost the whole city together to hear the word of God."*
5. Acts 13:44 - *"And the next Sabbath day came almost the whole city together to hear the word of God."*
6. Acts 13:48 - *"And when the Gentiles heard this, they were glad and glorified the word of the Lord."*
7. Acts 13:49 - *"And the word of the Lord was published throughout all the region."*

Notice, too, that in verse 43 Paul and Barnabas preached

"persuading them to continue in the grace of God."

If preaching were not necessary, there would have been no need for persuasion.

Nor was it merely halfhearted declaration. It was red-hot, evangelistic, urgent preaching. Paul pleaded with the lost to receive Christ (Acts 13:38, 39). He warned them of the consequences of rejection (Acts 13:40, 41). He also held them personally accountable for the sin of rejection (Acts 13:46, *"ye put it from you"*).

This section clearly highlights the crucial role of preaching in evangelism. The Gospel is spread not only through miraculous displays of God's power, but also through faithful preaching and personal witness.

Paul and Barnabas' obedience to God's call to proclaim His message resulted in countless souls being saved and the Word of the Lord being spread throughout the region. Fervency and urgency should most certainly accompany the preaching of the gospel.

- The Word describes itself as a - Hammer
- The Word describes itself as a -Fire
- The Word describes itself as a - Sword

Jeremiah 23:29; Hebrews 4:12-14

- If I say I'm preaching and someone doesn't feel "hammered" I'm not preaching!
- If I say I'm preaching and someone doesn't feel "lit" I'm not preaching!
- If I say I'm preaching and someone doesn't feel "pierced" I'm not preaching!

PREACH PREACHER!

Victorious Evangelism
Reaches the Hearts of Sinners

Imagine stepping into the bustling city of Corinth, a place teeming with life but also lost in spiritual darkness. This is where Paul, a humble messenger of Christ, found himself. Amidst the grandeur of temples dedicated to pagan deities and the noise of everyday commerce intertwined with less savory activities, one might wonder, how could a message of hope and redemption possibly take root here? Yet, it's in this setting that we witness the power of faith and the boundless potential of victorious evangelism. The story of Paul in Corinth is not just a historical account; it's a testament to the unyielding spirit of those called to share their faith.

Paul was met with a divine encouragement that speaks volumes to all who endeavor to live out their calling in challenging environments:

"For I am with thee, and no man shall set upon thee to hurt thee: for I have much people in this city" (Acts 18:10).

This heartfelt statement illuminates the essence of God's unchanging promises regarding His never ending presence.

But who were these "much people" in a city seemingly blind to the truth? They were there, hidden in plain sight, their hearts yet untouched by the message of salvation. They represented the untapped potential of a city that, on the surface, seemed lost. It's a powerful reminder that beneath the veneer of indifference, hostility, or paganism, there are souls yearning for meaning, truth, and redemption.

This description challenges us to look beyond the immediate, the visible, and the tangible. It compels us to ask ourselves, are we ready to unlock our potential as instruments of change? Are we prepared to venture into our own "Corinth's," armed with nothing but the gospel message, faith, and the assurance that we are not alone in our quest?

God's work through Paul in Corinth is a call to action. It's an affirmation that no effort in His name is in vain. Despite the apparent hopelessness, there was a plan, a divine strategy to reach those hearts shrouded in spiritual blindness. This story serves as a beacon, illuminating the path for all who wish to live out their calling, to empower, and to transform.

Are you ready to answer the call? To step into your own Corinth, knowing that your labor will bear fruit, that you are part of a larger purpose? This is the essence of victorious evangelism – a journey not of solitary endeavor but of collective transformation and empowerment. It's an invitation to unlock your potential and to live out your calling, supported by the unwavering promise: "I have much people in this city."

In reflecting on this story, we find not only inspiration but a blueprint for integrating faith into our professional and spiritual lives. The question then becomes, how will we respond? How will we use our lives as platforms for ministry, to reach the hearts of those still searching in the darkness?

The story of Paul in Corinth isn't just a narrative from the past; it's a living, breathing call to action. It invites us to step into the arena of faith, armed with the knowledge that our efforts are backed by the highest power. In this mission, we are never alone.

God Graciously Invites Sinners to Trust Christ

The Apostle Paul had another dream in which he heard a man from Macedonia, standing and begging him to come over and help them. Immediately after receiving this vision, Paul set out for Europe and came to Philippi (Acts 16:9-12). There he found Lydia who was by the riverside worshiping God. She received his message and was saved. Those who were in Mars' Hill also heard the message of Jesus Christ. There was a mixture of reactions, but some responded to the invitation and "believed" (Acts 17:34).

Who can forget the warm response that Paul received from those at Berea? Though they studied hard and long, having all their questions answered by God's Word through Paul, when they were finished studying, *"many of them believed"* (Acts 17:12).

In each case God was the One who did the saving. He takes all the glory through the initiative of evangelism. We do not go forth to win people to Christ because we are good or clever at apologetics. What is true of Paul must be true for us – our sufficiency is of God (2 Corinthians 3:5).

As we proclaim the gospel, let us do so with the assurance that God has much people in every place. We may be reaching out to folks who seem far away from Christ, but remember – God knows His own and will bring them to faith. Therefore, keep on preaching! Keep on witnessing! Keep on giving out gospel tracts! Keep on inviting the lost to meetings where the gospel is faithfully proclaimed! We can do so with the guarantee that God has His people and will call them by His grace.

The Power of Persuasion in Evangelism

In Acts 13:43, we see Paul and Barnabas persuading their listeners to continue in the grace of God. This demonstrates the power of persuasion in evangelism, the ability to convince someone through reasoning, revelation, and evidence.

Effective persuasion requires a combination of knowledge, passion, and empathy. As Christians, we must have a deep understanding of the gospel message and be able to articulate it with conviction and compassion. We should also seek to understand the perspectives and struggles of those we are sharing with, in order to tailor our message and approach accordingly.

But ultimately, it is the power of the Holy Spirit that brings about true persuasion and conversion. We can plant seeds and water them with our words, but without the work of the Spirit, there can be no growth.

In evangelism, we may face resistance or apathy from those we share with. But like Paul, we must persevere in our persuasion, trusting in God's plan and His ability to bring people to faith. We must also remember that it is not our abilities or techniques that save souls, but the power of God working through us.

God extends an open invitation to every sinner, encouraging each one to come and find rest for his soul in Jesus. This invitation is not limited by any conditions, as the call is to *"whosoever believeth"* (John 3:16), emphasizing that anyone who believes in Him shall not perish but have everlasting life.

Similarly, the promise of *"whosoever drinketh"* (John 4:14) illustrates the offering of the living water, which Jesus explains will become in them a spring of water welling up to eternal life. This makes it clear that the grace and salvation offered by God are accessible to all, without exceptions.

Hence, we can eagerly and honestly proclaim the gospel of saving grace to the entire world, assuring everyone that this message of hope and redemption is available to each person willing to accept it. By embracing this truth, we can participate in the spread of this transformative message, contributing to a world more aware and receptive of the boundless love God offers through Jesus Christ.

God Powerfully Convicts the Sinner
through His Word

In a moment that transcended time, Peter stood before a gathered crowd during Pentecost, delivering a message so powerful that it pierced the hearts of all who listened. Imagine feeling the weight of your actions so profoundly that you're left asking,

"What must I do to be right again?"

This was the impact of Peter's words, as recorded in Acts 2:37. The term "pricked" hardly does justice to the intense awakening experienced by the audience. It wasn't a mere nudge towards reflection but a deeply moving, soul-stirring conviction brought about by the divine truth of God's Word—a spiritual awakening so profound it could only be described as being stabbed with the truth, revealing the depth of one's own sin and the desperate need for redemption.

This incident illuminates a critical role of the Holy Spirit; to convict individuals of their sins, leading them towards righteousness and ultimately, judgment. While hearing the Word might stir a general awareness of sin, it's the deeper, more personal conviction by the Holy Spirit that transforms hearts and lives. Witnessing this doesn't always lead to salvation, as some resist this call to change, despite feeling its life-altering impact.

Salvation emerges as a beacon of hope within this complex interplay of divine conviction and human response. It is underscored throughout the New Testament that belief in the Lord Jesus Christ is the pathway to salvation. Echoing the clarity of Paul's words,

"Believe on the Lord Jesus Christ and thou shalt be saved" (Acts 16:31)

comes the reminder that this salvation is a matter of grace—undeserved, unearned, and freely given by God. This is beautifully encapsulated in Ephesians 2:8-9, emphasizing that salvation is through faith, not from our works, lest anyone should boast. It's about recognizing one's own inadequacy and helplessness in sin, and wholeheartedly believing in Jesus Christ as the savior who bore the penalty for these sins.

True faith extends beyond mere intellectual acceptance; it

involves a heartfelt commitment to Jesus Christ. It's an invitation to place your trust, your very life, into the hands of the Savior provided by God. Romans 10:13 captures this essence, highlighting that belief unto righteousness comes from the heart.

In this description of conviction and salvation, we see a powerful demonstration of God's love and mercy. It beckons us to reflect, to ask ourselves if we are merely listeners of the Word or if we allow it to penetrate our hearts, leading us to a place of transformation and redemption. Are we open to the convicting power of the Holy Spirit, allowing it to guide us towards the truth of salvation? It's a call to unlock our potential, to live out our calling not just in words, but through a profound, personal faith in the grace of God.

In conclusion, victorious evangelism is not measured by the number of souls won but by the faithfulness in carrying the message of the gospel and the power of the Holy Spirit in transforming lives. The Acts of the Apostles and the Epistles convey a clear message that evangelism, underpinned by the grace of God, the conviction of the Holy Spirit, and a deep, personal faith in Jesus Christ, holds the potential for profound spiritual renewal and salvation. It requires a heart willing to listen, a spirit ready to be convicted, and a life prepared to be transformed.

The accounts of Paul, Barnabas, Peter, and others testify to the resilience, passion, and unwavering trust in God's promise needed to pursue the Great Commission. Their experiences underscore that while challenges and resistance are inevitable, the outcome is in God's hands. The power of evangelism lies in its proclamation of hope, the offer of redemption, and the invitation to a relationship with God through Jesus Christ.

Thus, victorious evangelism is characterized by its reliance on the Holy Spirit to convict and convert, its celebration of the grace offered to all humanity, and its commitment to sharing the truth of

God's Word with compassion and humility. As we reflect on these principles, we are reminded of our role in God's redemptive plan and encouraged to actively participate in spreading the gospel, knowing that through our faithful witness, God can work mightily to bring individuals to a saving knowledge of Him. In this, we find our victory; not in numbers, but in the joy of seeing even one soul come to find eternal life through faith in Jesus Christ.

Chapter 6

Evangelistic Methodology

T he Jesus Revolution Movement, which emerged in the late 1960s and early 1970s, marked a significant period in the history of evangelical Christianity, particularly within the United States. It arose during a time of profound social and cultural upheaval, characterized by the Civil Rights Movement, anti-Vietnam War protests, and a burgeoning counterculture that challenged traditional values. This movement represented a radical departure from conventional church culture, adopting a more informal and contemporary approach to worship and community engagement. It sought to reconcile the message of Christianity with the issues and language of the younger generation, thereby addressing the growing disenchantment among youth towards institutionalized religion.

Key figures in the Jesus Revolution included pastors like Chuck Smith of Calvary Chapel, who opened his church to the influx of disenchanted youth, and Lonnie Frisbee, an influential evangelical preacher and charismatic figure who played a pivotal role in drawing the hippie population to the movement. Their approach combined traditional evangelical theology with a more relaxed, communal worship style that resonated with the youth of that era.

Among the notable conversion stories were those of individuals deeply entrenched in the counterculture—drug users, musicians, and activists—who found a new sense of purpose and community within the movement. Their testimonies highlighted the transformative power of faith, not only on a personal level but also in their ability to impact the broader society positively.

One of the most emblematic activities of the Jesus Revolution was the practice of mass public baptisms, which served as both a symbolic and public declaration of faith for new believers. The movement's baptisms were not confined to traditional church settings but instead often took place in natural bodies of water, such as oceans and rivers, making the act of baptism both a personal and communal experience. The most iconic of these events were held at Pirates Cove in Corona Del Mar, California, where hundreds, sometimes thousands, of individuals were baptized by leaders of the movement, including Chuck Smith, Lonnie Frisbee, and later, Greg Laurie. These baptismal services were a testament to the widespread impact of the Gospel Message, as individuals from diverse backgrounds and communities came together in a public profession of their faith. The visual and emotional impact of these mass baptisms, conducted in the backdrop of nature, further solidified the movement's appeal to the youth, emphasizing a return to the basics of faith and community.

The legacy of the Jesus Revolution Movement is still evident in today's evangelistic culture, particularly in the continuing emphasis on contemporary worship styles and the use of media and technology to disseminate the Christian message. It has also influenced the church's approach to social issues, encouraging a more engaged and compassionate response to the needs of the wider community. The movement underscored the importance of adaptability and cultural relevance in evangelism, principles that continue to guide modern evangelical practices.

In recent years, there's been a marked increase in interest in how to effectively spread the Christian faith. Church leaders and religious workers travel far and wide to conferences, workshops, and weekend training sessions to learn new strategies that draw large audiences, hoping these efforts will lead to a thriving congregation. The idea often circulated, whether by design or accident, is that a church's success in evangelism can be measured by its ability to draw a crowd and by the numbers it reports.

Many young pastors and those leading ministries, motivated by tales of booming churches nurtured by innovative practices, drink the Kool-aid and are keen to adopt these strategies in pursuit of similar success. Sometimes, the local church leadership feels pressured to match or surpass the attendance figures of other congregations, with the underlying message being that a smaller gathering signals failure. As God's church,

> "We are called to complete one another, not compete with one another." ~ Dr. Bill Claypoole

Attracting a large number of attendees doesn't automatically mean that genuine spiritual transformation is taking place. It's true that the church today is trying out evangelistic approaches that are unprecedented, and this isn't necessarily a problem. Indeed, it's crucial for churches to avoid becoming stagnant, sticking to outdated programs when fresh approaches could serve their mission better. But any new methods introduced should be evaluated against the teachings of the Bible - a process that involves examining these strategies through the lens of scriptural principles.

The New Testament, while not providing a checklist for every potential evangelistic tactic, offers guidelines and principles that can help Christians assess not just these strategies, but all aspects of their Christian walk. Unfortunately, it appears that some leaders within the Christian community have not thoroughly assessed the methods being used in their evangelistic efforts against these biblical standards. In the haste to achieve success, some practices that dishonor God and can be detrimental to the faithful are occasionally adopted.

It's essential for churches to remember that the goal of evangelism is not merely to increase numbers but to foster genuine faith and spiritual growth. This means prioritizing methods that are in harmony with God's word over those that simply promise quick results. In doing so, churches can ensure that their evangelistic efforts are both effective and respectful of the principles laid out in Scripture.

Theological Premises

Theological premises are the foundational beliefs that inform and guide evangelistic methodology. In other words, they shape how Christians understand and approach sharing their faith with others. These premises are essential because they not only influence the methods used but also determine the ultimate goal of evangelism.

The Belief in a Personal God

One of the core theological foundations of evangelistic methodology is the belief in a personal God, who is not distant or detached, but deeply engaged and interactive with the world. Christian evangelism profoundly roots itself in the conviction that

God exists, not as an abstract concept, but as an active, living presence in the lives of individuals. This foundational belief underpins the entire approach to evangelism, steering it towards a direction that prioritizes the cultivation of a personal relationship with God. Rather than focusing solely on disseminating doctrinal knowledge or theological facts about God, evangelism places significant emphasis on inviting individuals to experience a meaningful, personal connection with Him. This approach to evangelism highlights the importance of personal testimony and lived experience in faith conversations, aiming to demonstrate the transformative power of a relationship with God in one's life.

The Centrality of Jesus Christ

Another core theological foundation of evangelistic methodology emphasizes the central role of Jesus Christ in the process. This core belief is deeply embedded in the doctrine of salvation, which posits that establishing a correct relationship with God is only possible through Jesus Christ. Consequently, this truth dictates that the most effective evangelistic methods are those that concentrate on narrating the story of Jesus' life, His sacrificial death, and triumphant resurrection. These elements are presented as the pivotal means through which salvation can be attained. Evangelistic strategies are, therefore, designed to not only inform but also to inspire individuals with the transformative power of Jesus' message, encouraging them to embrace this path to spiritual redemption.

The Authority of Scripture

The authority of Scripture stands as a pivotal theological foundation profoundly influencing evangelistic methodology. As Christians we realize that the Bible is not merely a collection of texts, but the inspired Word of God, holding the ultimate authority over beliefs, faith, and practice. This belief in the divine inspiration and authority of Scripture shapes evangelistic efforts, as Christians are motivated to share their faith with others.

Consequently, evangelistic methods frequently involve sharing and explaining the truths found in the Bible to non-believers, in hopes of illuminating the transformative power of God's Word. Engaging with Scripture, Christians aim to communicate its relevance and offer an understanding that leads towards faith. Through this approach, evangelism becomes a bridge for conveying the profound truths found in a relationship with Christ that is grounded in the authoritative foundation of Scripture.

The Sinfulness of Man

The understanding of human sinfulness and the profound need for redemption forms a fundamental theological cornerstone that profoundly influences evangelistic methodology. The Bible teaches that all humans inherit sin from the moment of birth and, as a result, find themselves inherently separated from God due to this condition. This pivotal belief not only shapes but deeply informs the strategies and approaches towards evangelism. It underscores the paramount importance of individuals recognizing their own spiritual brokenness and the urgent need for God.

Evangelistic methods are carefully designed to not only communicate the Gospel Message but also to incorporate a potent call to repentance. This involves a heartfelt recognition of one's sinfulness and an earnest invitation for individuals to turn their lives towards God, seeking His forgiveness and aiming for reconciliation. Such an approach doesn't merely aim to convert individuals on a superficial level but seeks to promote a profound internal transformation. It emphasizes the personal account-ability of each individual in nurturing and maintaining their rela-tionship with God, highlighting the life-altering impact of recognizing one's sins and fully surrendering one's life to God's will.

Moreover, this methodology fosters a space where individuals are encouraged to reflect on their lives, recognize their imperfec-tions, and understand the liberating power of God's love and mercy. By doing so, it not only facilitates a deeper understanding of one's spiritual state but also opens the pathway for genuine spir-itual renewal and growth. Through this process, evangelism tran-scends the realm of mere religious recruitment and becomes a journey towards spiritual liberation and fulfillment, grounded in the acknowledgment of human frailty and the infinite grace of God.

The Role of the Holy Spirit

The role of the Holy Spirit plays a pivotal role in shaping evangelistic methodology, a concept deeply rooted in Christian theology. According to scripture, the Holy Spirit is not merely a passive presence; it is the divine force actively responsible for convicting individuals of their wrongdoing and sin. This convic-tion is not to condemn but to gently guide individuals towards the path of salvation through faith in Jesus Christ. This fundamental belief underscores the indispensable role of the Holy Spirit in the process of conversion.

The Bible declares that the Holy Spirit convicts the world of sin, righteousness, and judgment. This role is pivotal, not only in the individual's heart but also in shaping evangelistic strategies as Christians seek to partner with the Holy Spirit. The strategy involves more than just the spoken word; it is about creating an environment through prayer and spiritual guidance where the Holy Spirit can work effectively in people's hearts.

Through prayer, fasting, and a deep reliance on the guidance of the Holy Spirit, evangelism becomes a collaborative effort between God and believers. This partnership is geared towards drawing individuals towards a profound and personal relationship with God that is grounded in His grace, love, and mercy. Evangelists and missionaries are thus encouraged to lean not on their own understanding or persuasive skills but to trust in the Holy Spirit to prepare the hearts of those they are reaching out to. This approach ensures that the message of the Gospel is conveyed not in mere words, but with a demonstration of the Spirit's power.

In summary, the Holy Spirit's role in evangelism is multifaceted, from convicting and guiding to empowering believers to share the Gospel effectively. This understanding shapes a methodology that is both spiritual and strategic, aiming for the heart transformation of individuals through the power of divine intervention.

These theological premises not only guide how Christians approach evangelism but also underscore its ultimate goal - to lead individuals into a personal relationship with God through Jesus Christ. This goal is rooted in the belief that knowing and experiencing God's love and grace is the most significant need of every human being. Therefore, evangelistic methodology aims to share this message in a way that is respectful, relevant, and loving.

Apostolic Practice

Have you ever wondered how the early Christians spread their faith so effectively? It's fascinating that when we look into the New Testament, it doesn't lay out a detailed plan or specific methodologies for evangelism. Rather than focusing on the tactics, the spotlight shines brightly on the message being shared and the individuals delivering it.

In the sacred gatherings of the early believers, their priority was to connect with God through prayer and worship. They understood something profoundly important: the success of sharing their faith depended entirely on God's intervention. This belief wasn't just theoretical; it was deeply ingrained in their actions. For instance, in Acts 4:29-33, we see them earnestly praying for God to empower His Word and bless their efforts to spread His message[1].

This reliance on divine support highlights a critical aspect of their approach to evangelism. They recognized that no amount of human planning or strategy could substitute for the need for God's presence and power in their work. Their faith compelled them to seek God's guidance and blessing above all else.

Isn't there something incredibly empowering about this? It reminds us that in our endeavors—whether they're in business, ministry, or our personal lives—the key to impactful outreach lies not in our own abilities but in seeking alignment with God's will and provision.

Imagine applying this principle today. How would our projects, initiatives, and interactions change if we prioritized seeking God's direction and strength? It's an invitation to unlock our potential, not by relying solely on our strategies but by living out our calling with a dependence on God's power to make our efforts fruitful.

This perspective encourages us to look beyond our own capabilities and to lean into a faith that empowers and guides. In doing so, we open the door to making a profound impact, guided by the same divine support that fueled the early church's mission.

The Five Principal Methods of Early Church Evangelism

The early church employed at least five principal methods used by the Apostles and early believers in their evangelistic ministry. Let's look at them:

Holy Spirit Anointed Preaching

The apostles and early Christians were not just believers in the transformative power of Jesus Christ; they were fervent preachers, dedicated proclaimers of eternal life that can be found only through faith in Jesus Christ. The term kerygma, which translates to "the thing preached," is frequently used to describe their passionate proclamations. Interestingly, God has chosen what the world perceives as the *"foolishness of preaching"* as a divine tool to extend salvation to those who are willing to believe (I Cor. 1:21).

Paul explicitly ties the concept of the gospel to the *"preaching of Jesus Christ"* (Rom. 16:25), highlighting the inseparable connection between the message and the messenger. In the times of the New Testament, a "herald" or kerux in Greek, played a crucial role as one who delivered official proclamations to the public, a title that the New Testament aptly assigns to preachers. Demonstrating the importance of this role, Paul shares that he was *"ordained a preacher"* (I Tim. 2:7), indicating a divine commission to carry forward this sacred duty.

It's crucial to understand that the approach of the apostles was not to engage in casual conversation or to simply exchange religious opinions with those dwelling in ignorance and darkness. The essence of "preaching," as they practiced it, was to make authoritative declarations. This was not about tentatively announcing or searching for truth in uncertainty. Rather, it was about boldly proclaiming the completed work in Christ, a definitive declaration of salvation and redemption.

Moreover, the word used for "evangelizing" is sometimes translated as "preaching" in the King James Version. For instance, Acts 17:18 describes how Paul *"preached unto them Jesus and the resurrection."* This was not merely sharing information; it was conveying the exhilarating news of Christ's victory over sin and death, a message that bore the power to transform lives. Paul and the early Christians took this message across various settings, engaging diverse audiences, making preaching a principal method of spreading the gospel. Through this proclamation of a finished work in Christ, they were able to reach out to multitudes, offering them the hope and the promise of eternal life. This practice of preaching, deeply rooted in conviction and divine commission, was central to the early Christian mission and remains a cornerstone of Christian ministry today.

Divinely Inspired Teaching

Teaching serves not only as a method of imparting knowledge but also as a powerful vehicle for evangelism. Reflecting on his time in Ephesus, Paul recounted to the elders how he utilized public teaching as a platform to spread the core doctrines of repentance and faith (Acts 20:21), effectively using it as a means to introduce the gospel to new ears. It's likely that thousands of children have encountered the gospel for the first time through their Sunday School teachers, or perhaps via instructors of released-time classes or during the sessions of a school-day children's club.

Moreover, small groups and home Bible classes have proven to be a fertile ground for sowing the seeds of faith in many hearts. These examples underscore the variety of teaching environments that can be harnessed by the Holy Spirit to guide individuals toward a profound faith in Christ. Each setting offers unique opportunities to connect with learners on a personal level, allowing the message of the gospel to be tailored and delivered in the most impactful way.

Spirit-Led Witnessing

Believers are commonly referred to as "witnesses" within the texts of the epistles, an interesting term that carries profound implications. Additionally, the notion of being a "witness" extends even to God in certain scriptural passages, such as Philippians 1:8 and Romans 1:9, where the phrase *"God is my witness"* is notably used. This terminology encompasses both the capacity to testify to verifiable truths, those facts known with certainty to the witness, and the ability to express personal convictions with fervor. Intriguingly, the origin of the word "witness" in Greek is "martus," which directly informs the English term "martyr." This association arose presumably because those who fervently testify to their convictions often face persecution or suffering as a consequence.

In the context of Christian doctrine, Christ himself designated believers as witnesses to the Savior, entrusting them with the mission to testify to His life, death, and resurrection. This is vividly illustrated when Paul, preaching in Antioch in Pisidia, spoke emphatically of the death and resurrection of Christ. He highlighted that these monumental events were not shrouded in secrecy but were observed by many, making these observers "witnesses" to the unfolding divine plan, tasked with sharing the "good news" of salvation as detailed in Acts 13:26–32.

This role of being a witness for Christ is not a passive or symbolic appointment but a dynamic call to action. Every believer is charged with the responsibility to be a witness for Christ, to share the transformative work of Christ for sinners, and to offer a personal testimony of what Christ has accomplished in their own lives. The apostles themselves modeled this with great zeal, as evidenced in Acts 4:33, where it's stated,

"And with great power gave the apostles witness of the resurrection of the Lord Jesus: and great grace was upon them all."

This demonstrates that witnessing is not confined to the realms of the church or formal religious gatherings but extends into everyday life - in the marketplace, offices, streets, schools, homes, and every conceivable place where God's presence manifests.

Furthermore, evangelism and the act of witnessing are not reserved for a select few within the Christian community, but rather, it is the blessed privilege and duty of every believer. This universal call emphasizes the importance of personal testimony in the life of a Christian, underscoring that through sharing one's faith and experience of God, believers participate in the broader mission of the church to spread the gospel. This act of witnessing thereby becomes a powerful tool for spiritual growth and communal strengthening, as believers affirm their faith and encourage one another through their shared testimonies and experiences of God's transformative power in their lives.

Power Packed Praying

What profound and miraculous effects are brought forth through the power of prayer! Among these, not the least is the salvation of a soul that was once lost. It is a profound duty and privilege to intercede before God on behalf of our lost loved ones, friends, and associates, beseeching for their salvation with fervent hearts. The apostle Paul himself, burdened with a heavy heart for his people, exemplified this as he wrote: "Brethren, my heart's desire and prayer to God for Israel is, that they might be saved" (Rom. 10:1). In his deep longing, Paul was praying earnestly for the salvation of his kinsmen according to the flesh, showcasing a model of intercession that we, too, would do well to follow.

Following Paul's example, we cannot underestimate the power of pouring out our hearts to God on behalf of those who have yet to find their salvation. Through our prayers, God is capable of removing the veil of spiritual blindness, enabling lost souls to gain an appreciation for the incomparable glories of Christ, and ultimately leading them to place their trust in Him for their eternal salvation.

Furthermore, there is immense value in "praying under the unction of the Holy Spirit." This concept reminds us that we are not alone in our prayers; we are supported and guided by the Holy Spirit itself. We are comforted by the assurance that "the Spirit also helpeth our infirmities: for we know not what we should pray for as we ought: but the Spirit itself maketh intercession for us with groanings which cannot be uttered" (Rom. 8:26). This divine assistance in prayer is a profound mystery, wherein the Holy Spirit intercedes for us in ways that transcend human understanding, ensuring that our prayers align with the will of God.

In embracing this deeper communion with God through prayer, guided by the Holy Spirit, we open ourselves to be conduits of God's grace, pleading for the salvation of souls with a fervency that can move mountains. The practice of such earnest prayer, steeped in love and propelled by the Holy Spirit, stands as a testament to the boundless power of faith and the limitless compassion of God for His creation.

Many a soul has been saved because some praying man or woman was faithful in interceding before God. The writer of the Epistle to the Hebrews exhorts us:

"Wherefore he is able also to save them to the uttermost that come unto God by him, seeing he ever liveth to make intercession for them." (Heb 7:25)

It's a comforting assurance that Christ, our great High Priest, continues to intercede for us and for the salvation of all who come to Him. This should also serve as a reminder that we, as His followers, have been entrusted with the same responsibility to intercede on behalf of others.

Holy Spirit Led Writing

God will pour it through us if we let Him. When God called me to share the wisdom He had imparted over the last forty years, specifying that my mission was to write, my initial response was, "I don't feel qualified to author a book." However, I soon realized that a divine inspiration accompanies such a heavenly mandate for writing.

Throughout history, the pens of God's servants have crafted powerful appeals aimed directly at the hearts of the unsaved. Among these, perhaps the most profound is the Gospel of John, a masterpiece of divine inspiration designed to reach out to the lost sinner. This Gospel eloquently declares,

"But these are written, that ye might believe that Jesus is the Christ, the Son of God: and that believing ye might have life through his name" (Jn. 20:31)

offering a path to salvation and eternal life.

While the message of the gospel permeates the New Testament, John's Gospel stands out for its explicit evangelistic intent. Crafted with care by John, it has served as a cornerstone for evangelistic efforts for centuries. Since its inception, countless tracts, booklets, and books have been penned, all with the aim of unpacking the gospel's deep truths and pressing upon the unsaved the critical importance of placing their faith in Jesus Christ, God's Son.

These written works have played a pivotal role in the spread of Christianity, ensuring that the message of salvation reaches far and wide, across different cultures and generations. Written ministry, with its ability to convey complex ideas and timeless truths, remains a vital tool in evangelism. It not only educates but also inspires faith in those searching for meaning, offering them a chance at a new life anchored in the hope and redemption found in Jesus Christ.

Scriptural Guidelines for Evangelism Methods

The methodology of evangelism, deeply rooted in Scripture, is guided by several fundamental principles. Below are key Scriptural principles that govern effective evangelistic efforts, along with relevant scriptures:

- **Go and Make Disciples**: The Great Commission, a fundamental tenet of Christian faith, as recorded in *Matthew 28:19-20*, stands as the paramount directive for evangelism and outreach. It explicitly calls upon believers to go forth into the world, transcending geographical and cultural boundaries, to make disciples of all nations. This involves not only baptizing them in the name of the Father, the Son, and the Holy Spirit but also teaching them to observe and live by all the commands that Christ has given. This commission underscores the importance of spreading the teachings of Jesus Christ and expanding the community of believers globally.

- **Preach the Word**: At the heart of evangelism lies the crucial task of proclaiming God's Word. It's not merely about sharing one's own beliefs but about conveying the truths found within the scriptures. The Apostle Paul, in 2 *Timothy* 4:2, provides timeless advice for all who wish to spread the Christian faith: "Preach the word; be prepared in season and out of season; correct, rebuke and encourage—with great patience and careful instruction." This directive underscores the importance of being ready to share the gospel at all times, utilizing it to guide, correct, and inspire others, all while exhibiting patience and providing thorough instruction.

- **Live by Example**: The effectiveness of evangelism is significantly enhanced when believers not only share the Gospel with their words but also demonstrate its power and grace through their daily actions and decisions. *Philippians* 2:15-16a specifically encourages believers to be luminaries in the world, shining brightly like stars, by holding firmly to the word of life. This approach emphasizes that living a life that reflects the teachings of the Gospel can profoundly influence others more than words alone. It's about embodying the principles of love, compassion, and integrity that Jesus taught, thereby inspiring others to explore the faith through the example set.

- **Practice Humility and Gentleness**: The guidance from *1 Peter* *3:15-16* emphasizes the critical need to adopt an attitude of gentleness and respect when engaging in evangelism. It's not just about sharing your faith, but doing so in a manner that reflects the humility and kindness taught by Christ. This approach ensures that your conscience remains clear, and it offers a powerful contrast to any slanderous accusations thrown your way. By embodying these values, you present a living example of Christian behavior that can leave naysayers feeling ashamed of their negative judgments.

- **Pray for Opportunities and Boldness to Share the Gospel**: As highlighted in *Colossians* *4:3-4*, prayer plays a pivotal role in the process of evangelism. It's essential to ask God not only to create opportunities for spreading His word but also for the courage and boldness to seize these moments effectively. This passage emphasizes the importance of praying for clarity in communication, ensuring that the message of the gospel is delivered in a way that can be easily understood and received by others.

- **Depend on the Holy Spirit**: The indispensable role of the Holy Spirit in evangelism is monumental, as it equips and empowers believers to witness with extraordinary effectiveness. The Holy Scripture, particularly *Acts* *1:8*, explicitly states that believers are endowed with power when the Holy Spirit descends upon them, enabling them to be compelling witnesses to the furthest corners of the earth. This divine empowerment is crucial for overcoming the challenges of spreading the Gospel and ensuring that one's testimony resonates deeply with those who hear it.

- **Seek the Lost with Compassion**: This principle is deeply rooted in reflecting the mission of Jesus to seek and save those who are lost. As illustrated in *Luke 19:10*, this approach to evangelism is driven by a profound compassion for the lost. It emphasizes the importance of reaching out to those who have not yet found their way, drawing inspiration from the compassionate example set by Jesus Christ. This guiding principle encourages believers to actively pursue those in need of spiritual guidance with a heart full of compassion and understanding, mirroring the love and dedication Jesus himself showed.

- **Use of Parables to Convey Kingdom Truths**: Jesus frequently employed parables, which are simple stories or analogies, to illustrate and communicate profound spiritual truths in a manner that was accessible to everyone, regardless of their background or level of understanding. This teaching method, exemplified in passages such as *Mark 4:33-34*, showcases how storytelling can be a powerful and effective tool in evangelism. By using relatable stories or analogies, the complex and transformative messages of the gospel can be conveyed in a way that resonates with a wide audience, facilitating a deeper understanding and connection with the teachings of Christianity.

- **Partnering with Others**: The concept of evangelism was always envisioned as a collaborative effort rather than a solitary journey. This is beautifully encapsulated in *Ecclesiastes 4:9*, which declares, "Two are better than one, because they have a good return for their labor." This principle is not just theoretical but was practically applied by Jesus Himself when He sent out His disciples in pairs to preach. This method not only provided moral support and companionship but also reinforced the message's credibility and effectiveness, illustrating the profound impact of partnership in spreading the gospel.

- **Exercise Patience and Persistence**: The art of evangelism is not for the faint of heart. It often demands a deep reservoir of patience and an unwavering commitment to persistence, as vividly illustrated in the Parable of the Sower (*Matthew 13:3-23*). This parable teaches us a valuable lesson about the nature of spreading the Word of God. It reminds us that not every seed we plant will instantly find fertile ground and flourish. Some seeds may fall on rocky paths or among thorns, facing challenges that prevent their growth. However, among these, there will be seeds that find good soil, take root, and produce a bountiful harvest. This metaphor serves as a powerful encouragement for anyone dedicated to sharing their faith. It underscores the importance of continuous effort, despite the obstacles and setbacks that might arise. By consistently sowing the Word of God, being patient, and not losing heart, we contribute to a future where those seeds can grow into something beautiful and sustaining.

The Scriptural guidelines for evangelism methods presented above offer a multifaceted approach for spreading the Gospel effectively and meaningfully. Each principle, rooted in the teachings and practices of Jesus Christ, illuminates the path for believers to follow as they engage in the holy mission of evangelism.

By integrating practices of humility, prayer, reliance on the Holy Spirit, compassion, storytelling, partnership, and patience into our evangelistic efforts, we do more than share a message; we embody the living testament of God's love and salvation.

These guidelines are not merely strategies but are reflections of the heart and character of Christ, inviting all who hear to not only receive the Word but to encounter the transformative power of His love. Therefore, as we proceed in our evangelistic endeavors, may we do so with the fullness of heart and the empowerment of the Spirit, trusting in the Lord to bring forth the increase in His perfect timing and will.

Effective Evangelism Strategies for Today

In alignment with scriptural methodologies, contemporary evangelism strategies must be both innovative and rooted in the timeless wisdom of the Bible. Below are strategies that reflect biblical principles and are adapted for effectiveness in today's world:

- **Leveraging Social Media for Gospel Outreach**: In an era dominated by digital communication, social media platforms present unparalleled opportunities for sharing the Gospel.

Platforms such as Facebook, Instagram, and Twitter can serve as modern-day marketplaces, where believers can share compelling content related to faith, Scripture, and personal testimonies. This approach aligns with the scriptural principle of going where the people gather, as Jesus did, using contemporary forums for engagement and discourse.

- **Engaging in Service and Social Justice Initiatives**: Jesus' ministry was marked not only by preaching but also by acts of service and compassion towards the marginalized and needy. Today, Christians can embody the Gospel through involvement in community service and social justice initiatives. By addressing tangible needs and advocating for societal change, believers can demonstrate the love of Christ in action, opening doors for meaningful conversations about faith.

- **Interfaith Dialogues and Cultural Exchanges**: Promoting respectful and thoughtful dialogues with individuals of different faith backgrounds or no religious affiliation can foster mutual understanding while providing a platform for sharing the Christian faith. This strategy is reminiscent of the Apostle Paul's approach in Athens (Acts 17), where he engaged with the culture and beliefs of the locals as a bridge to introduce the Gospel.

- **Developing Personal Relationships**: While mass evangelism efforts have their place, the Bible places significant emphasis on personal relationships for discipleship and witnessing. Investing in friendships and showing genuine interest and care for individuals can create natural opportunities to share the Gospel. This one-on-one approach mirrors Jesus' interactions with Nicodemus, the Samaritan woman at the well, and Zacchaeus.

- **Utilizing Technology for Virtual Bible Studies and Fellowships**: The accessibility of video conferencing tools has opened new avenues for conducting Bible studies and fellowship meetings virtually, allowing for participation from individuals globally. This method upholds the scriptural value of communal study and edification, adapting it to the digital age.

- **Creative Arts and Storytelling**: Similar to Jesus' use of parables, harnessing the power of stories, music, drama, and visual arts can be a poignant way to convey spiritual truths and stir hearts towards contemplation and faith. Creative expressions of the Gospel can bridge cultural and linguistic barriers, making the message of Christ accessible to diverse audiences.

These strategies, although modern in their application, are deeply rooted in the principles and practices exemplified by Jesus and the early church. They encourage believers to engage with the world in relevant and meaningful ways, using every available tool and platform to spread the hope and truth of the Gospel. As we continue to adapt and innovate our evangelistic efforts, may we always keep in mind the ultimate goal of bringing glory to God and leading others to salvation through Jesus Christ.

More Evangelism Idea's

The strategies outlined previously exemplify how ancient scriptural methodologies can be adapted for effective evangelism in today's global and digital landscape. Continuing in this vein, the following strategies further embody the timeless principles of Biblical evangelism, ensuring their relevance and efficacy in contemporary society:

- **Prayer Walks in Local Communities**:
  Organizing prayer walks in neighborhoods or cities not only serves as a physical manifestation of faith but also as a method for believers to actively seek God's presence and blessing in their communities. This strategy echoes the Biblical principle of prayer as a powerful tool in witnessing and spiritual warfare.

- **Hosting Q&A Sessions on Faith via Webinars or Live Streams**: Leveraging technology to host question and answer sessions can provide a non-threatening platform for curious seekers and skeptics to explore the Christian faith. This modern approach parallels the Biblical tradition of open discourse and teaching in the synagogues and public places.

- **Collaborative Community Impact Projects**:
  By partnering with local organizations or other churches, believers can undertake projects that have a

tangible impact on their communities, such as environmental sustainability efforts, educational initiatives, or homeless outreach. This strategy is reminiscent of the early church's commitment to service and community welfare.

- **Digital Storytelling and Testimonial Sharing**: Utilizing blogs, podcasts, and video platforms to share personal stories of faith transformation can resonate deeply with a diverse online audience. This method reflects the scriptural emphasis on testimony as a means of witnessing God's grace and power in one's life.

- **Online Discipleship and Mentorship Programs**: Creating structured programs for new believers to learn about the faith and grow spiritually through digital media addresses the need for discipleship in the digital age. This mirrors the Biblical model of mentorship and teaching within the faith community.

- **Multicultural Worship Services and Events**: Organizing worship services that celebrate cultural diversity within the Christian community can be a powerful demonstration of the unity and inclusivity of the Gospel. This approach draws on the New Testament's vision of a multi-ethnic, multicultural church body.

- **Faith-Based Podcasts and Radio Shows**: Leveraging the reach and accessibility of podcasts and radio shows to discuss topics related to Christianity, share devotionals, or explore theological issues can effectively engage listeners in their daily routines. This medium allows for the continuation of the Christian tradition of preaching and teaching through modern technology.

By incorporating these strategies into their ministry, believers can effectively witness to the Gospel in a manner that is both respectful of scriptural traditions and responsive to the realities of the contemporary world. These approaches, by bridging the gap between ancient truths and modern contexts, underscore the enduring relevance and transformative power of the Christian message.

The Story of David Wilkerson & Teen Challenge

In the late 1950s, the evangelistic story of David Wilkerson, a small-town preacher from Pennsylvania, became a seminal example of outreach and ministry transforming lives in urban settings. Moved by a photo in *Life Magazine* of several young gang members on trial for murder, Wilkerson felt a divine call to minister to the troubled youth of New York City. With little more than faith and determination, he set out for the notoriously dangerous streets of Times Square and the surrounding neighborhoods, an area plagued by gangs, drugs, and violence.

Wilkerson's ministry in New York began with significant challenges. He faced hostility and skepticism from the very people he sought to help, as well as from those who doubted his methods. Yet, his persistent efforts to reach out to gang members began to bear fruit, most notably in the conversion of Nicky Cruz, a gang leader from the Mau Maus. Cruz's transformation from a life of violence to one of faith and service is a highlight in Wilkerson's ministry, showcasing the power of relentless love and persistence in the face of adversity.

This remarkable encounter and the subsequent work among the city's youth led to the establishment of Teen Challenge, an organization dedicated to helping troubled teens and adults over-come addiction and other life challenges through faith-based solu-tions. The story of David Wilkerson's ministry, including his impactful interaction with Nicky Cruz, was later popularized in Wilkerson's book, "The Cross and the Switchblade", underscoring the profound effects of evangelical outreach in urban contexts. This narrative not only illuminates the pivotal role of faith in reha-bilitation but also exemplifies how singular acts of evangelism can evolve into widespread movements for community transformation.

In closing, the methodologies discussed in this chapter encourage believers to undertake the work of evangelism with both courage and sensitivity, always reliant on the Holy Spirit's guid-ance. By embodying the principles of Christ's love and employing varied strategies to meet the evolving challenges of the world, Christians can continue to make an impactful difference in indi-vidual lives and communities. Thus, the call to evangelism is not just a duty but a privilege, offering an opportunity to participate in the divine work of bringing hope and salvation to a world in need.

Chapter 7

Grace and Evangelism Today

Grace and evangelism are two important concepts in Christianity. As a Christian, it is essential to understand the meaning and significance of these two terms. Grace refers to the unmerited favor of God towards humanity. It is through grace that we are saved from our sins and have eternal life with God. This concept is central to the message of Christianity as it emphasizes the love and mercy of God towards us.

Evangelism, on the other hand, is the act of sharing the gospel or good news of Jesus Christ with others. It is an essential aspect of living out our faith as Christians. In fact, Jesus himself commands us to go and make disciples of all nations (Matthew 28:19). Evangelism allows us to spread the message of God's love and salvation to others, inviting them to experience the same grace that we have received.

When it comes to evangelism today, there are various methods and approaches that Christians can use. Some may prefer traditional forms of evangelism such as street preaching or handing out tracts, while others may utilize modern technology and social media platforms. No matter the method, the goal remains the same – to share the love and message of Jesus Christ with others.

However, as we engage in evangelism, it is important to remember that it should always be done with grace and love. Our words and actions should reflect the grace that God has shown us. We should never force or manipulate others into accepting our beliefs, but instead, we should share the gospel in a respectful and compassionate manner.

Moreover, evangelism should not be limited to just sharing the message verbally. Our lives should also reflect the grace of God in our actions and relationships with others. As 1 Peter 3:15 says,

"But in your hearts revere Christ as Lord. Always be prepared to give an answer to everyone who asks you to give the reason for the hope that you have. But do this with gentleness and respect."

Our lives should be a testimony to God's grace, drawing others towards Him.

Therefore, grace and evangelism go hand in hand in the work of winning the lost. As we receive God's grace, it compels us to share the good news with others in a loving and respectful manner.

The History of Evangelism and Grace

Evangelism and grace have been integral components of the Christian faith since its inception. In the early days of Christianity, it was predominantly spread through personal conversations and testimonies, as well as through public preaching by apostles and disciples. As the church grew in numbers, organized efforts such as missionary journeys were used to share the message with people from different regions.

Throughout history, various methods and strategies have been employed for evangelism, but the message of God's grace has remained consistent. The Protestant Reformation in the 16th century saw a revival of grace-centered theology, emphasizing that salvation is a gift from God through faith alone.

In more recent times, evangelism has taken on different forms such as mass revivals, door-to-door evangelism, and Christian music concerts. The rise of technology has also opened new avenues for sharing the gospel, such as online sermons and social media outreach.

Regardless of the method used, grace remains at the core of evangelism – a reminder that salvation is not earned but freely given by God's grace.

Evangelism, derived from the Greek word 'euangelion,' meaning 'good news,' refers to the act of preaching the Gospel to share the message of Jesus Christ. Grace, on the other hand, is a foundational concept in Christian theology that denotes unmerited mercy and love from God towards humans. Together, these concepts form the core of the Christian mission – to spread the saving grace of God through Jesus Christ.

The significance of evangelism and grace extends beyond historical or doctrinal importance; it permeates the fabric of contemporary spiritual life, guiding moral decision-making, community building, and personal growth among believers.

Theoretical Foundations of Grace

The theological underpinnings of grace vary among different Christian denominations, yet they coalesce around the principle of divine benevolence that surpasses human understanding and merit. The concept of grace highlights the generous, free gift of salvation and forgiveness through Jesus Christ, enabling believers to reconcile with God.

The interpretations of grace across various Christian denominations underscore the theological diversity within Christianity. Each tradition approaches the concept of grace with nuances that reflect its broader doctrinal commitments:

- **Catholicism:** The Catholic Church teaches that grace is a gift from God that enables humans to participate in His divine life. It distinguishes between actual grace, which refers to God's interventions and support for transient acts, and sanctifying grace, which is a stable disposition that perfects the soul itself to enable it to live with God, to act by His love. Sacraments are considered primary means through which God dispenses His grace.

- **Eastern Orthodoxy:** In Eastern Orthodox theology, grace is the energies of God Himself, not created but uncreated. It is through these energies that God makes Himself known to us and brings us into communion with Him. The concept of theosis or deification is central, highlighting the process of becoming more like God through His grace while maintaining that God's essence remains incomprehensible and inaccessible to humans.

- **Protestantism:** Within Protestantism, interpretations of grace vary widely, but generally, grace is understood as the unmerited favor of God towards sinners. For Lutherans, grace received by faith alone is central to salvation. Calvinists emphasize irresistible grace, suggesting that God's grace is given freely without regard to human merit and cannot be refused. Methodists, conversely, espouse prevenient grace, affirming that God's grace works in everyone's lives to lead them towards salvation, which they can then accept or reject.

- **Baptists:** Baptists commonly hold to the belief in sola gratia, meaning salvation comes through grace alone, not through any human effort. They emphasize a personal relationship with Jesus Christ as the means by which grace is received for salvation.

- **Pentecostalism:** For Pentecostals, grace is not only about salvation but also empowerment for living a holy life and for ministry. They emphasize the importance of the baptism in the Holy Spirit, through which believers receive power to witness and serve God effectively.

- **Anglicanism:** Anglican doctrine views grace as both a gift from God for undeserved forgiveness through faith in Christ and an enabler of human cooperation with God. They maintain a balance between God's sovereignty in dispensing grace and human agency in responding to that grace.

These perspectives on grace highlight the rich diversity of Christian thought. They reflect differing emphases on God's sovereignty, human free will, the means by which grace is received, and the effects of grace in the believer's life. Despite these variations, the common thread among all Christian traditions is that grace is a fundamental aspect of Christian faith and mission.

The Call to Evangelism

As Christians, we are called to share the message of salvation through Jesus Christ with others. This call to evangelism is rooted in the Great Commission (Matthew 28:18-20), where Jesus commands His disciples to go and make disciples of all nations. This commission is not just for a select few but for all believers, as the message of God's grace is meant to be shared with everyone.

Evangelism can take many forms – from one-on-one conversations to large-scale events – and each believer may have a different approach based on their gifts and personal experiences. Still, the underlying motivation remains the same – to share God's love and grace with others.

In a world that is increasingly divided and hurting, the message of grace is more relevant than ever. It offers hope, forgiveness, and reconciliation in a broken world. As we continue to spread the good news of Jesus Christ through evangelism, may we do so with humility, compassion, and love for all. May we always remember that it is God's grace, not our own efforts or merits, that brings salvation to all who believe.

The advent of the digital age has significantly transformed methods of evangelism, marking a pivotal change in how the Gospel is shared across the globe. With the introduction of a wide spectrum of new mediums, including social media platforms, digital churches on livestream, and even virtual congregations within the Metaverse, the landscape of religious outreach has expanded beyond traditional boundaries. This shift necessitates a delicate balance between adhering to the timeless, traditional evangelistic principles that have guided generations and harnessing innovative approaches to effectively reach contemporary audiences, who are increasingly immersed in digital environments.

As we delve into an exploration of how these changes impact the way Christians fulfill their evangelical mission today, let us be cognizant of both the opportunities and challenges presented by digital platforms. The goal is to understand how the essence of evangelism can be preserved while adapting to a rapidly changing world, ensuring that the message of the Gospel continues to resonate with individuals from all walks of life in this new digital era and resulting in their decisions to accept Jesus as their Savior.

Grace in Everyday Life

Have you ever considered how the concept of grace can extend far beyond the realm of theological debate and become a tangible force in our daily lives? In a world that increasingly values action over words, understanding grace is not just about acknowledging a divine gift but about translating that acknowledgement into acts of kindness, forgiveness, and unconditional love towards both ourselves and those around us. This transformation of personal and communal life through the practice of grace can serve as a profound testament to the power of faith in action.

When we talk about God's grace, we are referring to something incredibly powerful—something that doesn't just change us on the inside but pushes us to make a real difference in the world around us. How, then, can we bridge the gap between the theory of grace and its practice in our everyday lives? The scripture reminds us,

"*For it is by grace you have been saved, through faith—and this is not from yourselves, it is the gift of God*" (Ephesians 2:8).

This passage invites us to live out our calling with a heart full of gratitude, showing kindness and compassion in every interaction.

Yet, as we strive to embody this grace in our actions, we encounter challenges, especially in the realm of evangelism. In today's world, where skepticism and indifference often greet religious messages, how can we effectively share our faith without alienating those we wish to reach? It's about striking a delicate balance, demonstrating genuine concern for both the spiritual and temporal welfare of others without being seen as merely tricking them.

Overcoming these challenges necessitates a deep understanding. It requires us to engage in evangelism not through a lens of superiority, but from a place of openness and genuine respect for others. If individuals sense a lack of empathy or respect from you, they will be closed off to your message. Hence, it's crucial to demonstrate, not merely articulate, the transformative impact of faith. This involves showing how faith can enable us to fulfill our potential and elevate those around us.

Are you ready to unlock your potential and live out your calling by integrating faith into every aspect of your life? Remember, it's not just about what we say; it's about what we do with the grace we've been given. By approaching each day with an open heart and a willingness to act with kindness and love, we can not only transform our own lives but also make a significant impact on our community and beyond.

Case Study
The Woman at the Well

One of the most compelling narratives of conversational evangelism in the Bible is found in the account of Jesus and the Samaritan woman at Jacob's well (John 4:4-42). This story epitomizes the power of grace-filled dialogue in breaking down barriers and transforming hearts.

Jesus, on His journey, stops at a well in Samaria, a place where Jews typically would not tread due to deep-seated prejudices against Samaritans. Here, He encounters a woman drawing water at midday, an unusual time suggesting she may have been avoiding the social stigma from her community. In initiating conversation, Jesus transgresses cultural norms, demonstrating a willingness to engage with those ostracized by society.

The dialogue that unfolds between Jesus and the woman is profound and multi-layered, beginning with a simple request for a drink of water. Jesus uses this mundane exchange as a gateway to deeper spiritual discussions, gradually revealing His knowledge of her personal life and her search for something beyond mundane existence. He offers her "living water," leading to a conversation about true worship and ultimately revealing His identity as the Messiah.

The woman's initially skeptical response turns to intrigue and, eventually, belief, as evidenced by her leaving her water jar behind to tell her townspeople about her encounter with Jesus. This act of leaving the jar symbolizes her transformation from a life of shame and seeking to one of purpose and evangelism. Her testimony leads many in her community to believe in Jesus, showcasing the ripple effect of conversational evangelism.

This story exemplifies the essence of grace in evangelism. Jesus meets the woman where she is, physically and spiritually, without judgement, and speaks to her deepest needs and longings. It is a testament to how genuine encounters, rooted in compassion and respect, can transcend historical enmities and personal shortcomings, leading to profound personal transformation and wider community impact.

Case Study
Jesus and Zacchaeus

Another profound illustration of grace and evangelism is the encounter between Jesus and Zacchaeus, as narrated in the Gospel of Luke (Luke 19:1-10). Zacchaeus, a chief tax collector in Jericho, was a man despised by his community. His occupation made him wealthy, albeit at the expense of his fellow citizens, through the oppressive tax system enforced by the Roman authorities. This background sets the stage for a remarkable episode of transformation that underscores the power of grace and the impact of personal evangelism.

As Jesus entered Jericho, He drew the attention of a large crowd. In this crowd was a tax collector named Zacchaeus who sought to catch a glimpse of the man he had heard so much about. Given Zacchaeus's short stature, he climbed a sycamore tree for a better view. This act, in itself, was a departure from the dignity expected of a man of his status, indicating his deep curiosity and spiritual hunger. Upon reaching the spot, Jesus looked up, pinpointing Zacchaeus amidst the foliage and the crowd. In a move that shocked those present, Jesus addressed him directly, instructing Zacchaeus to come down and announcing His intention to stay at his house.

This gesture of inclusion and acknowledgment was radical. Jesus chose to engage with a person deemed unworthy by society, breaking through the barriers of prejudice and ostracization. The effect of this encounter on Zacchaeus was transformative. He received Jesus joyfully, and the ensuing interaction led to a profound moral and spiritual awakening within him. Zacchaeus publicly vowed to give half of his possessions to the poor and to restore fourfold to anyone he had defrauded. This pledge went beyond the requirements of the law, reflecting a heartfelt repentance and a sincere desire to rectify the wrongs of his past.

The story of Jesus and Zacchaeus exemplifies the power of grace and the essence of evangelism. Jesus's willingness to engage with Zacchaeus, without condemnation but with an open invitation to change, facilitated a radical transformation. Zacchaeus's response to grace was not merely internal; it manifested in actions that sought to bring justice and restitution to those he had wronged. This true Bible story highlights how grace, when coupled with genuine repentance and tangible action, can reconcile individuals to their community and restore relationships broken by injustice and greed. Through this story, we are reminded of the inclusive nature of Jesus's ministry and the redemptive possibilities of grace, underscoring the profound impact that personal encounters and conversations can have in the realm of evangelism.

Case Study
Evan Roberts and the Welsh Revival

The Welsh Revival (1904-1905), led by Evan Roberts, stands as one of the most extraordinary instances of communal transformation within the history of Christianity. Roberts, a young coal miner turned preacher, became the catalyst for a revival that swept through Wales, dramatically altering the social and spiritual fabric of the country.

The revival began after Roberts, following a profound personal spiritual experience, felt compelled to share his message of repentance and salvation through Christ. His initial meetings, characterized by intense prayer, confession of sins, and passionate preaching, ignited a fire that rapidly spread across Wales. The impact on the community was unprecedented. Taverns, once bustling centers of social life, closed their doors due to a lack of patrons, as men and women alike turned to prayer and worship, foregoing their previous indulgences.

One of the most curious effects of the revival was on the working animals of the region. It is reported that mules, used in the mines, had to be retrained to understand commands. The miners, having experienced profound conversions, ceased using the profane language they previously employed to direct the animals. This anecdote symbolically underscored the depth of change that had permeated every aspect of Welsh life.

The revival was not without its critics, yet the tangible outcomes were undeniable. Families were restored, debts were repaid, and entire communities were unified under a banner of spiritual renewal. Perhaps the most telling impact of the revival was the number of conversions; within six months, it is estimated that over 100,000 people received Christ. This period of revival left a lasting legacy on Wales, evidencing the transformative power of the Holy Spirit when people collectively seek a deeper relationship with God.

The story of Evan Roberts and the Welsh Revival serves as a powerful testament to the impact of fervent prayer and devout faith on society. It highlights how a spiritual awakening can transcend individual hearts, revitalizing entire communities and altering the course of history.

Case Study
The Great Awakening in Colonial America

The Great Awakening, a religious revival that swept through the American colonies in the mid-18th century, represents another historic instance of spiritual renewal profoundly influencing society. This revival emerged in a context of declining piety and growing secularism amongst the colonies. Itinerant preachers, the most notable being George Whitefield and Jonathan Edwards, traversed the colonies, delivering powerful sermons that emphasized personal salvation, the necessity of a new birth in Christ, and a direct, emotional connection with God.

Unlike the structured and doctrinal approach typical of the time, these sermons appealed to listeners' emotions and urged a personal experience of faith. The impact was remarkable, leading to widespread conversions, reinvigoration of church congregations, and the establishment of new schools and colleges dedicated to religious education, such as Princeton and Dartmouth.

The Great Awakening broke down denominational barriers, encouraged a spirit of ecumenical unity among Christians, and significantly diminished loyalty to the established Church of England, thereby laying a spiritual groundwork for the American Revolution. It fostered a sense of shared American identity and democratic ideals, as it promoted the belief that all people are equal before God, which translated into social and political spheres.

The Awakening's influence extended beyond the religious realm, instilling in the American people a sense of empowerment and individualism. It helped to democratize American religion and set the stage for the future shaping of the American ethos. The revival demonstrated the power of spiritual awakening to forge a nation's identity, unify its people, and reshape its cultural and religious landscape.

* * *

In conclusion, the deep exploration of grace and evangelism uncovers their unrelenting relevance and pivotal role in sustaining the Christian faith across different generations. This chapter has been meticulously written with the noble intent of motivating individuals and entire communities to foster a culture that deeply values grace and wholeheartedly commits to the practice of evangelism. By doing so, we ensure that these ageless principles continue to steer and enrich the Christian journey in profound ways.

The future trajectory of grace and evangelism rests securely in the hands of those who are prepared to engage with these concepts in a thoughtful and reflective manner, applying them with diligence and devotion in their personal lives and wider communities. We find ourselves in a critical moment in time, one that is in dire need of another divine intervention from heaven above. The world is crying out for a revival—a profound resurgence of faith and spirituality that results in an undeniable connection with their Creator-God. Therefore, as faithful Christians, we are called upon to rethink and rejuvenate our approach to sharing God's boundless love and grace in an increasingly complex and diverse global landscape through the powerful mediums of Evangelism and Grace.

The task ahead involves not only reaching out with the timeless message of the Gospel but doing so in ways that resonate with the modern audience. It's about bridging the gap between ancient biblical truths and contemporary societal challenges, making the message of grace and the call to evangelism as compelling and relevant today as it has ever been. As we navigate these efforts, it's crucial to remember that our strength and success lie not in our strategies or eloquence but in the transformative power of the grace we preach and the divine support that guides our evangelistic endeavors.

Chapter 8

New Testament Church Evangelism

The evangelistic efforts described in the New Testament were deeply rooted in its churches, which played a pivotal role in the spread of the gospel. The outcome—new believers—were not just added to the numbers but were integrally incorporated into these faith communities. These churches were not mere buildings or gatherings; they stood at the very heart of New Testament evangelism, entrusted with the monumental task of spreading Christ's teachings and his gospel to the far corners of the world.

For evangelism that truly honors God and aligns with His purpose, a profound and clear understanding of the New Testament church's nature, its functions, and its central role in the life of believers is absolutely imperative. Unfortunately, today's perspective on the local church is often clouded by widespread misconceptions, leading to a dilution of the kind of evangelism envisaged by the New Testament. These misunderstandings can create barriers that obstruct the flow of genuine evangelistic fervor, distancing believers from the original blueprint laid out in the scriptures.

Contrary to how it might be viewed in contemporary settings, evangelism in the New Testament was not an isolated or peripheral activity. It was, in fact, a core aspect of the church's mission and purpose—a mission deeply interwoven with the very identity of the Christian community. As followers of Christ, we are called and tasked with the noble mission of sharing the good news of salvation with those yet to hear it. This mission, as presented in the New Testament, is a collective duty of the church, rather than an endeavor meant for isolated individuals. It's a communal calling that reflects the unity and purpose of the body of Christ.

In this chapter, we will delve deeper into the New Testament's teachings concerning the local church's pivotal role in evangelism. Our journey will take us through an exploration of scriptural insights and practical examples that highlight how early Christians understood and lived out this mission. By closely examining these foundational principles, we aim to emulate this divinely guided model of evangelism, aspiring to fulfill our calling in a manner that honors God and effectively reaches those in need of the gospel's transformative power. Through this exploration, it is our hope that readers will gain a richer, more nuanced understanding of the church's mission to evangelize, inspiring a renewed commitment to this vital aspect of Christian faith and practice.

Evangelism and the Local Church

In exploring the foundations of Christian faith, it's crucial to understand the role that local churches play as central pillars in upholding and spreading the truth. The New Testament, specifically in 1 Timothy 3:15, refers to the local church as the *"pillar and ground of the truth."* This metaphor beautifully captures the idea that local congregations are not just gatherings; they are guardians of faith, tasked with preserving, defending, and sharing the truth within their communities and beyond.

Consider the powerful example set on the Day of Pentecost. After Peter delivered a moving sermon, many accepted Christ as their Savior, were baptized, and joined the ranks of a newly formed local congregation (Acts 2:41). This wasn't a mere addition to a group but a transformation into a unified body of believers, a tangible representation of Christ's church on Earth. Being part of this congregation meant something profound; it signified belonging, commitment, and shared responsibility. This is further evidenced when members of this early church were chosen to serve, demonstrating organized participation and leadership within the community (Acts 6:3).

A pivotal moment in the New Testament that underscores the foundation and authority of the church occurs in Matthew 16:18, where Jesus tells Peter,

> *"And I tell you that you are Peter, and on this rock I will build my church, and the gates of Hades will not overcome it."*

This passage signifies a profound theological and ecclesiological principle. The term "ekklesia," used here for "church," conveys the notion of a called-out assembly or congregation, indicating a distinct and purposeful gathering of believers.

By referring to Peter as "rock," intertwined with the promise to build His church, there lies a dual layer of interpretation and application.

- Firstly, it underscores Peter's role and, by extension, the apostles' foundational role in the early church.

- Secondly, and more critically, it points to Christ Himself as the ultimate foundation upon which the church is established (1 Corinthians 3:11).

Thus, the church's foundation is not merely human leadership or authority but the divine, unchangeable truth of Christ's lordship and gospel being established in the earth.

This exchange between Jesus and Peter not only delineates the church's inception but also marks the indomitable nature of the church against all adversarial forces. The "gates of Hades" will not prevail against it, symbolizing the church's victory over death and evil through the resurrection power of Christ. This affirmation begets the inviolable security and eternal significance of the church in God's redemptive plan.

Drawing parallels from ancient Greek city-states, where the term "ekklesia" denoted a specific assembly of citizens, it becomes clear that the concept of the church as a "called-out ones" was always meant to embody structure and purpose. Just as citizens participated in civic affairs, so does Christ's ecclesia engage actively in spiritual matters, guided by His teachings. This structure is not about rigid formalities but about fostering a thriving, evangelistic community, as seen in the early Jerusalem church. Its growth and effectiveness in spreading the Gospel underscored the vital link between internal organization and outward mission (Acts 6:7).

This structured approach to faith is further solidified by Jesus' promise of the "Keys of the Kingdom," empowering the church to enact God's will on Earth as it is in Heaven (Matthew 16:19). It's a reminder that the church's role isn't passive; it's a dynamic force for change, equipped to make significant impacts both spiritually and socially.

Therefore, understanding the local church's responsibility

highlights a call to action for believers. It invites us to reflect on how we, too, can contribute to our congregations and communities. How can we uphold the truth in today's world? How can we, through our local churches, become more effective in our mission to spread the Gospel?

Evangelism and the Ascension Gifts

Upon His ascension, Christ gifted His Church with leadership gifts, as outlined in Ephesians 4:11. These gifts are known as the Ascension Gifts—Apostle, Prophet, Evangelist, Pastor, and Teacher—were bestowed to build and educate the New Testament church, of which we are members.

The Greek word used for "gifts" here is *doma,* which means divine or spiritual gift. It underscores the fact that these gifts are not humanly acquired, but a direct bestowal from Christ Himself. Moreover, their purpose is to equip believers in their roles within the church and facilitate its growth (Ephesians 4:12-13).

The Role of the Apostle: The term "apostle" originates from the Greek word "apostolos," which translates to "one who is sent forth." Historically, apostles have played a crucial role in the early Christian church by establishing new congregations, disseminating the teachings of Jesus Christ, and spreading the Gospel far and wide. Their work involved not only preaching and teaching but also providing spiritual guidance and mentorship to emerging spiritual leaders and believers, nurturing the growth of the early Christian community. The work of the Apostle still continues today.

Moreover, the early Apostles were responsible for writing many of the New Testament scriptures, which have become foundational texts for Christian doctrine, worship, and moral guidance. These writings include gospels, letters, and apocalyptic literature that address a wide range of theological, ethical, and practical issues. Through their epistles and narratives, the Apostles convey the teachings of Christ, offering encouragement, correction for doctrinal errors, while providing instructions for church governance and Christian living.

Their contributions have had a lasting impact on Christianity, shaping its beliefs, practices, and community life. The Apostles' dedication to their mission, willingness to face persecution, and commitment to spreading the message of salvation have left an indelible mark on the history of Christianity and continue to inspire Christians around the world to this day.

The Role of the Prophet: In religious contexts, a prophet is considered a messenger chosen and inspired by God to serve as His spokesperson. Prophets play a crucial role in delivering God's messages and revelations to His followers, guiding them through their faith. The role of prophets in the New Testament focuses on:

- Edification, which involves building up and strengthening the church,
- Exhortation, to encourage and motivate the believers to adhere to their faith, and
- Comfort, offering reassurance and solace to the community of believers in their times of need.

It's important to distinguish the evolving role of prophets from the Old Testament to the New Testament. In the Old Testament, prophets were often tasked with providing direction and correction to the people, acting as intermediaries between God and His people during times of disobedience or spiritual waywardness. They were instrumental in guiding the moral and spiritual direction of the community, often through warnings of divine judgment or promises of God's favor depending on the people's actions.

However, in the New Testament, the role of prophets underwent a significant transformation. The emphasis shifted towards nurturing and building up the Christian community in faith and practice. This change reflects the New Testament's broader theme of redemption and reconciliation through Jesus Christ, focusing on spiritual growth and encouragement within the church. Prophets in the New Testament era are thus seen as vital contributors to the spiritual well-being and development of the believers, using their divinely inspired insight to foster a deeper, more resilient faith among the followers of Christianity.

Furthermore, The introduction of Apostles and Pastors, tasked with correction and guidance (among other things) under the Holy Spirit's direction, prompted this change. Unlike the Old Testament era, where prophets bore these responsibilities, the roles of Apostle and Pastor were established to fulfill these duties in a new context. This shift underscores God's intent to make His guidance on correction and direction more relational than in the past.

The Role of the Evangelist: An evangelist is not just any ordinary person; they are individuals who have been uniquely gifted for a very special purpose – sharing the Gospel with those who have not yet been exposed to its life-changing message. These individuals are distinguished by a unique set of personality traits and spiritual giftings that enable them to excel in their calling.

First and foremost, they exhibit an exceptional level of zeal and enthusiasm for the Gospel, coupled with a deep love for people. This love fuels their desire to reach out and share the message of hope and salvation with those who are yet to know Christ. They are typically outgoing, able to easily connect with others on a personal level, which is crucial in breaking down barriers and building relationships.

In terms of spiritual giftings, evangelists are endowed with a remarkable ability to communicate. This is not limited to mere eloquence but includes the ability to convey complex spiritual truths in simple, understandable terms. They are adept at contextualizing the Gospel message, making it relevant to the audience's cultural and societal concerns without compromising its integrity. Additionally, evangelists are often graced with the gift of faith, enabling them to trust God for the miraculous, including the transformation of hearts and lives. This faith propels them to venture into areas others might consider too hard or resistant to the Gospel.

The effectiveness of evangelists also lies in their resilience and perseverance. They often face rejection and opposition, yet their commitment to their divine mission remains unshaken. This steadfastness is a testament to their character and their unwavering belief in the power of the Gospel to change lives.

Furthermore, effective evangelists exhibit a keen discernment, recognizing open doors and opportunities for sharing the Gospel. They are sensitive to the guidance of the Holy Spirit, knowing when to speak and when to remain silent, when to act boldly and when to wait patiently.

Collectively, these traits and giftings ensure that evangelists can fulfill their role in the body of Christ, contributing significantly to its growth and the spread of Christianity across the world. Their work, driven by love, faith, and perseverance, continues to be a vital component in achieving the Great Commission.

. . .

The Role of the Pastor: A pastor serves as a shepherd, teacher, and overseer of the local church. This integral role involves leading congregational services, providing spiritual guidance, and overseeing the administrative aspects of church operations. The personality of an effective pastor is multifaceted, embodying a unique blend of qualities that enable them to fulfill their pastoral duties with diligence and compassion.

Firstly, an effective pastor possesses a deep empathy and understanding towards others, which facilitates a nurturing and supportive environment for spiritual growth. This empathy is rooted in a genuine love for their congregation, allowing pastors to connect on a personal level and provide guidance and comfort in times of need.

Furthermore, effective pastors exhibit exceptional leadership skills, characterized by integrity, humility, and a servant-hearted attitude. These individuals lead by example, demonstrating a life of faith and obedience that inspires others to follow suit. They are also adept communicators, capable of conveying biblical truths in a way that is both accessible and relevant to their audience.

In addition to these interpersonal skills, effective pastors are resilient and adaptable, navigating the challenges of ministry with grace and determination. They are committed to their calling, showing perseverance in the face of adversity and maintaining a steadfast faith in God's provision and guidance.

Overall, the personality of an effective pastor is marked by a profound commitment to serving others, a deep-rooted faith in God, and a life that exemplifies the teachings of Scripture. Through their empathetic leadership, unwavering dedication, and spiritual insight, pastors play a pivotal role in the spiritual well-being and growth of the Christian community.

. . .

The Role of the Teacher: A teacher plays a pivotal role in guiding others through the complexities of sound doctrine and biblical principles. Entrusted with the significant task of imparting wisdom, they possess a profound comprehension of Scripture, coupled with a unique ability to elucidate its teachings. Their expertise allows them to render biblical truths in a manner that is not only relatable but also deeply relevant to the challenges and experiences of everyday life. Through their dedicated efforts, teachers enlighten, inspire, and foster a deeper, more meaningful understanding of spiritual principles among their students.

An effective Biblical teacher embodies a confluence of attributes that not only illuminate their profound respect and understanding of Scripture but also their dedication to conveying its teachings to others. Foremost among these attributes is a profound intellectual curiosity and a commitment to lifelong learning. This curiosity fuels their comprehensive study of the Bible, enabling them to explore the depths of its wisdom and to constantly seek further understanding of its teachings.

Critical thinking is another hallmark of an effective Biblical teacher. They possess the ability to analyze and interpret Scripture with discernment, distinguishing between different interpretations and understanding the historical and cultural contexts of biblical events. This analytical approach ensures that their teachings are grounded in sound doctrine and are relevant to the contemporary world.

Empathy and sensitivity are indispensable in the personality of a Biblical teacher. These traits allow them to comprehend the diverse backgrounds and needs of their students, facilitating teachings that resonate on a personal level. Their empathetic nature fosters an inclusive learning environment where questions and doubts can be voiced and explored without judgment, promoting a culture of open inquiry and mutual respect.

Patience and humility further characterize an effective Biblical teacher. Patience is necessary to guide students at varying levels of understanding and spiritual maturity, recognizing that growth in knowledge and faith is a gradual process. Humility, on the other hand, reflects the teacher's recognition of their role as a servant-leader, prioritizing the welfare and spiritual growth of their students above their own accolades or recognition.

Ultimately, an effective Biblical teacher's personality is underpinned by a fervent passion for the Scripture and a sincere desire to share its transformative power with others. Their teaching is not merely an academic exercise but a ministry and calling to nourish the spiritual lives of their students, encouraging them to live out biblical principles in their daily lives. Through their wisdom, compassion, and commitment, they cultivate a deeper, enduring engagement with the Bible among those they teach.

Together, these Ascension Gifts work in harmony to educate and equip the church for its ultimate purpose: making disciples of all nations (Matthew 28:19-20). This is the central call and mission of the church, rooted in Christ's Great Commission. Each member has a role to play in fulfilling this command, whether through evangelism, teaching, serving, or supporting the work of the church.

The local church is not just a gathering of believers but a divinely ordained institution with a purpose and structure. It is built upon the unshakable foundation of Christ and empowered by His Spirit to fulfill its mission in the world. As members of this body, we have a responsibility to actively participate in its work and make a meaningful impact in our communities. Let us strive to emulate the early church in its devotion to truth, unity, and mission, as we continue to grow and thrive under the guidance of Christ's Ascension Gifts.

Evangelism and the Local Church Pastor

One of the most crucial roles in the local church is that of the pastor, who serves as a spiritual leader and shepherd for their congregation. This includes not only guiding and nurturing existing believers but also actively reaching out to those outside the church through evangelism.

The call to evangelize is not just reserved for pastors, but it is a responsibility shared by all members of the church. However, the pastor's role is especially crucial in setting an example and equipping their congregation to confidently share their faith with others.

An effective local church pastor understands the importance of evangelism and actively encourages and supports their members in this endeavor. They teach and model the Gospel message, equip believers with practical tools for sharing their faith, and provide opportunities for outreach within the community.

Through their leadership, pastors not only impact the spiritual growth of believers but also play a vital role in expanding the reach and influence of the local church. As they faithfully fulfill this aspect of their ministry, they continue to build upon the foundation laid by Christ and advance His mission to make disciples of all nations.

Additionally, The term *"pastors and teachers"* found in Ephesians 4:11 is often misunderstood as referring to two distinct gifts. However, a closer examination of the text reveals that it actually denotes a single, unified role—the pastor-teacher. This particular understanding highlights that the qualities of pastoral care and teaching are intrinsically linked, rather than separate.

The pastoral heart, along with the ability to teach, is a gift that emanates from the risen Christ, underscoring its divine origin. This gift is not given to all but bestowed upon certain individuals by God. These chosen individuals are graced with a special ability that enables them to shepherd a flock of believers effectively. Shepherding, in this context, encompasses a wide range of responsibilities, including praying, guiding, nurturing, protecting, and teaching. This comprehensive approach ensures the spiritual well-being and growth of the congregation, highlighting the profound significance of the pastor-teacher role in the Christian faith.

Evangelism and a Maturing Congregation

One of the inevitable challenges that every congregation faces is the physical aging of its members. This issue goes beyond the spiritual maturation in faith, focusing instead on the temporal aspect of aging within the church body. The primary mission of the congregation remains unwavering: to shepherd its members towards the ultimate goal of making heaven their eternal abode. When a congregation begins aging, their departure often happens in clusters, which presents a distinct challenge to the overall church community.

As the congregation begins to age, it's crucial to address this demographic shift proactively. One of the most effective strategies to tackle this challenge head-on is through a vibrant and well-structured evangelism ministry. A dedicated evangelism effort not only supports the existing members but also plays a pivotal role in attracting new members of various ages. By fostering growth and inviting new individuals into the fold, the church can maintain its vitality and dynamism, even as some of its cherished members reach the end of their earthly journey and achieve their heavenly reward.

Adopting a philosophy of *"Honoring History, Reaching for Destiny"* can serve as a guiding principle during this transitional period. This approach emphasizes the importance of respecting and celebrating the rich legacy of the congregation while simultaneously striving towards a future filled with growth and spiritual fulfillment. By navigating this transition with care and strategic planning, the congregation can continue to flourish, ensuring that it remains a vibrant community of faith that honors its past and looks to the future with hope and determination.

Furthermore, the role of the pastor-teacher is crucial in the spiritual development of the congregation. They are tasked with the responsibility of ministering the Word of God so that the believers, or saints, will reach a state of perfection and maturity in their faith (Ephesians 4:12). The term *"perfecting"* in this context was historically used in a medical sense, referring to the careful setting of broken or dislocated bones. Similarly, this term is used in reference to pastoral ministry, highlighting the pastor's crucial role in teaching and preaching God's Word. Effective teaching of God's Word mends the broken and realigns the believer's life, enabling it to function at its highest capacity for the Kingdom.

Therefore, the diligent exposition and application of scripture effectively guide the saints towards a well-rounded and robust Christian life. In this way, the pastor-teacher serves as a vital facilitator for the spiritual maturation of the congregation, equipping them to effectively fulfill their roles in evangelism and ultimately bring glory to God. Overall, it is clear that the role of the local church pastor and the mission of evangelism are intrinsically intertwined and crucial for the growth and impact of the church community.

The saints are called to be edified *"for the work of the ministry"* (Ephesians 4:12), which means equipping them for effective service to God. This service is not limited to evangelism alone, though evangelism is undeniably a significant aspect of it. The concept of ministry here is broad, encompassing various forms of service that contribute to the building up of the Body of Christ. Each believer is encouraged to exercise a ministry for God, which hinges on the unique spiritual abilities bestowed upon them by the Holy Spirit.

"But the manifestation of the Spirit is given to every man to profit withal" (1 Corinthians 12:7)

emphasizes that these spiritual gifts are intended for the common good, to build and edify the church.

God's design for a congregation includes a beautiful tapestry of people endowed with diversified gifts. This diversity is not accidental but intentional, designed to meet the manifold needs within the church and beyond its walls. When these gifts are utilized, the congregation not only grows spiritually but can also experience growth numerically. As believers actively employ their gifts in service, they contribute to a vibrant church life, marked by dynamism and vitality. This vitality is a testament to the living Spirit at work within the community, transforming lives and drawing more people into the fellowship.

Moreover, the employment of diversified gifts within a congregation fosters a sense of unity and purpose. As members recognize and celebrate the varied contributions of each person, they learn to value the unique role they play in God's kingdom work. This understanding nurtures mutual respect and deepens the sense of community among believers. Consequently, a church that embraces and encourages the diverse ministries of its members not only evidences life and vitality but becomes a beacon of hope and a source of light in the community it serves.

* * *

In conclusion, New Testament church evangelism is a complex yet exceedingly rewarding endeavor that necessitates the active engagement of the entire body of believers, underpinned by the strategic leadership of the local church pastor. The pastor's role, bolstered by the Ascension Gifts, is indispensable in guiding the church through the evolving challenges of ministry and mission. By steadfastly focusing on the maturation of the congregation through sound teaching and fostering an ethos of evangelism, pastors lay a solid foundation for the church's enduring impact on both the local community and the world at large. This unified approach ensures that the New Testament church remains a beacon of hope, salvation, and transformation in an ever-changing world.

Chapter 9

Outreach Evangelism

Outreach Evangelism is a term often used in Christian circles to describe the act of sharing one's faith with others outside of a church setting. It involves actively reaching out to those who may not know about Jesus or have a relationship with Him, and sharing the good news of His love and salvation.

Evangelism itself comes from the Greek word *euaggelion*, which means "good news" or "gospel." This term was originally used to refer to the message that Christians share, but it has also come to encompass the act of sharing that message with others.

Outreach evangelism is an important part of the Christian faith, as it follows Jesus' command in Matthew 28:19-20 to *"go and make disciples of all nations."* It is a way for believers to live out their faith and fulfill their purpose in spreading the word of God.

There are many different methods and approaches to outreach evangelism, but the essence remains the same: to share the love of Christ with others and invite them into a personal relationship with Him. This can be done through various means such as personal conversations, community events, mission trips, and online outreach.

Ultimately, outreach evangelism is not about forcing one's beliefs onto others but rather sharing the good news in a loving and respectful manner. As stated in Colossians 4:5-6,

> "Be wise in the way you act toward outsiders; make the most of every opportunity. Let your conversation be always full of grace, seasoned with salt, so that you may know how to answer everyone."

Through this approach, Christians can effectively spread the message of God's love and bring more people into His kingdom.

One of the most effective ways to evangelize today is through music and worship events. These gatherings provide a welcoming and non-threatening environment for people to experience the love of God through music, prayer, and fellowship. It allows individuals to witness firsthand the joy and peace that comes from having a relationship with Jesus.

The Different Kinds of Music in Worship

Music plays a significant role in the act of worship and evangelism. It has the power to move hearts, stir emotions, and convey messages in a way that words alone cannot. In a worshipping church, there are different kinds of music that can be used to effectively share the message of Jesus.

- **Traditional Hymns:** These are songs that have been passed down through generations and are often accompanied by an organ or piano. They have a rich history in the church and can evoke nostalgia for those who grew up singing them. Traditional hymns also contain powerful messages of faith and can be used to convey the gospel to listeners.

- **Contemporary Worship Songs:** These are more modern songs that utilize a variety of instruments such as guitars, drums, and keyboards. They often have a more upbeat and energetic sound. Contemporary worship songs tend to use simpler language and repetitive lyrics, making it easier for non-believers to understand and connect with the message.

- **Gospel Music:** Originating from African American churches, gospel music is known for its soulful melodies and powerful lyrics that can move listeners to tears. It is deeply rooted in the Christian faith and can be a powerful tool for evangelism, as it connects with people on an emotional level.

Furthermore, there are many different worship styles internationally. Take Japan for instance. Their worship instruments are more heavily influenced by their traditional instruments, such as the koto and shakuhachi, creating a unique blend of traditional and contemporary sounds. This allows individuals to worship in a way that is culturally relevant to them while still conveying the message of Jesus.

In Jamaica and the islands, reggae worship is a popular style that incorporates elements of traditional reggae music with Christian lyrics. It has become a powerful tool for evangelism in these communities, as it speaks to the cultural identity and struggles of the people while also sharing the message of Jesus.

In the streets of our majors cities here in America a rap style is more effective in spreading the message of Jesus, particularly in urban communities where rap music is prevalent while southern gospel is more influential in rural areas. The diversity of worship music allows for a powerful outreach to individuals from all walks of life.

Still others need a quieter form of worship. They are often drawn to contemplative music, such as instrumental or choral pieces. These types of worship can be used to create a peaceful and reflective atmosphere, allowing individuals to open their hearts and minds to the message of Jesus.

So you see, evangelism is an important aspect of a worshipping church and can be done through various forms of music. By utilizing different styles and incorporating cultural influences, churches can effectively reach out to diverse audiences and share the love and grace of God. As the Bible says in Colossians 3:16,

> "Let the message of Christ dwell among you richly as you teach and admonish one another with all wisdom through psalms, hymns, and songs from the Spirit, singing to God with gratitude in your hearts."

Many Christians tend to limit God, believing He can only act in ways they are familiar with or approve of. To such individuals, I would remind you: God is not beholden to your expectations! He is God and He can move any way He chooses.

Outreach Evangelism

Evangelism must be done where lost people are. They will not be reached by simply sitting in a church building or among other believers. The Bible says in Matthew 9:37, "The harvest is plentiful, but the workers are few." This verse reminds us of the importance of actively going out into the world to share the message of Jesus.

Music and worship events provide a unique opportunity for this kind of outreach. They can be hosted in public spaces, such as parks or community centers, making it easier for non-believers to attend and experience the love of God. It also allows for conversations and connections to be made with individuals who may not have otherwise stepped foot inside a church.

In addition to music events, other forms of outreach through evangelism can include:

- Serving the community through volunteer work
- Hosting events for youth and families
- Supporting local missions and charitable organizations

Through these acts of service and outreach, individuals can see the love of God in action and be drawn to Him. As Christians, it is our duty to not only share the message of Jesus but also live it out in our daily lives.

The Impact of Music Evangelism
Hillsong Church

Hillsong Church, originating from a humble suburban Sydney church in Australia, has grown to become a global phenomenon, significantly attributed to its approach to worship through music. Founded by Brian and Bobbie Houston in 1983, Hillsong's transformation into an international entity showcases the power of music in worship and evangelism. The church's music ministry, known as Hillsong Worship, played a pivotal role in this growth. Their contemporary Christian music transcended local boundaries and reached a worldwide audience, offering a fresh and modern way to experience worship.

The impact of Hillsong's music on their growth cannot be overstated. Albums produced by Hillsong Worship, Hillsong United, and Young & Free have achieved gold and platinum status, winning multiple awards and drawing thousands to their concerts and conferences. This music, characterized by its anointed, uplifting melodies, and deeply spiritual lyrics, has not only generated a global following but has also been pivotal in introducing people to the Christian faith.

Hillsong's approach to using music as an evangelistic tool is evident in their annual conferences and worship services, which attract attendees from across the globe. The church leverages music to create an inclusive and engaging atmosphere, making it easier for people to connect with the message of the gospel. The widespread appeal of their music has also opened doors to mainstream media and platforms, further amplifying their reach and influence.

Today, Hillsong's music is a major evangelistic tool that continues to inspire and influence the contemporary worship culture worldwide. It underscores the church's mission to:

"reach and influence the world by building a large Christ-centered, Bible-based church, changing mindsets and empowering people to lead and impact in every sphere of life."

Through their music, Hillsong Church remains at the forefront of evangelistic outreach, demonstrating the enduring power of worship music as a catalyst for spiritual awakening and community building.

The Impact of Music Evangelism
Elevation Church

Elevation Church, founded by Pastor Steven Furtick in 2006 in Charlotte, North Carolina, stands as a paradigm of modern Christian evangelism, with Elevation Worship playing a central role in its outreach efforts. From its inception, Elevation Church has been characterized by rapid growth, both in attendance and in its impact, a development significantly supported by the innovative use of music in worship and evangelism.

Elevation Worship, the worship ministry of Elevation Church, has been instrumental in defining the church's identity and outreach strategy. Their music bridges the gap between traditional hymns and contemporary worship songs, creating a unique sound that resonates with a broad audience. This approach to worship music has not only fostered a deep sense of community among congregants but has also extended the church's evangelistic reach beyond its physical locations.

The evangelistic impact of Elevation Music is tangible in the numerous testimonies of individuals who have encountered the Gospel through their songs. Albums such as "Here as in Heaven" and singles like "O Come to the Altar" and "Do It Again" have become anthems of faith for many, drawing listeners into a deeper relationship with God. The lyrical depth, combined with compelling melodies, invites an encounter with God, encouraging both reflection and action.

Elevation Worship's presence extends well beyond the walls of Elevation Church, with their music being played in churches around the world. This global reach is amplified through platforms like YouTube and Spotify, where their songs garner millions of views and streams, illustrating the music's widespread appeal and its potential to touch hearts across cultural and geographical boundaries.

Furthermore, Elevation Worship's impact is also evident in their collaborations with other renowned Christian artists and worship movements, facilitating a cross-pollination of musical styles and evangelistic efforts. These collaborations have served to broaden the appeal of Elevation Music and by extension, the message of the Gospel it carries.

In conclusion, Elevation Church's story is one of rapid growth and expansive outreach, with Elevation Worship standing as a beacon of modern evangelism. Through their music, Elevation Church has managed to craft a distinctive voice in the realm of Christian worship, one that speaks directly to the hearts of believers and seekers alike. The fusion of compelling lyrics with contemporary melodies demonstrates the church's commitment to using every available tool to spread the Gospel, affirming the power of music as a catalyst for evangelization and spiritual renewal.

Marketplace Evangelism

In a world that often feels disconnected from its spiritual roots, the call to intertwine faith with every aspect of our lives has never been more pressing. Have you considered how your everyday life and spiritual beliefs could not just coexist but flourish together? This isn't a new concept; in fact, it finds its roots deep within the early days of Christianity, as depicted in the dynamic narratives of the book of Acts.

The early Christians didn't limit their sharing of the gospel to the four walls of a church. Instead, they ventured out, embedding their faith into the very fabric of society. Picture the scenes described in Acts 5:42 – the apostles teaching and preaching about

Jesus Christ *"daily in the temple, and from house to house."* They were not deterred by societal norms or legal actions against them (Acts 4:13–22), their message so compelling that Jerusalem itself was said to be *"filled with their doctrine"* (Acts 5:28). The gospel, according to Acts 8:4, was spread *"everywhere,"* reaching even the most unexpected places, from public discussions in great centers (Acts 17:22) to personal conversations on journeys and in jails. Such was their commitment that the apostle Paul boldly stated the gospel had been preached *"to every creature which is under heaven"* (Col. 1:23).

Why does this matter to us today? The challenge and opportunity for modern believers lie in realizing that evangelism and fulfilling our calling aren't confined to traditionally religious settings. Far too many communities remain untouched by the church's outreach, not due to a lack of need, but perhaps because of a limited perspective on how to connect with individuals where they are. It's a poignant reminder that the essence of sharing our faith isn't about drawing people into a physical building; it's about reaching out to them in their current circumstances—be it in schools, workplaces, or their homes. The Great Commission is a command to *"Go!"*

This approach demands creativity, courage, and conviction. It requires seeing every interaction in our daily lives as a chance to live out our faith, to demonstrate the love and hope found in Christ. It begs the question, are we ready to step out of our comfort zones and into our communities with the good news of the Gospel?

The task may seem daunting, but remember, the same Spirit that empowered the early church guides us today. It's about unlocking your potential to make a meaningful impact, to empower others through your actions and words, and live out your calling with unwavering faith. Just as the early Christians filled

Jerusalem with their doctrine, we too have the opportunity to infuse our sphere of influence with the transformative power of the gospel.

The Impact of Marketplace Evangelism
Kingdom Business Networks

The concept of Marketplace Evangelism is further exemplified through the initiative of the Kingdom Business Network (KBN). This network represents a vibrant community of Christian entrepreneurs and business professionals who are dedicated to integrating their faith with their business practices. KBN leverages the marketplace as a fertile ground for evangelism, embodying the principle that one's vocation can serve as a powerful medium for spreading the Gospel.

Members of the Kingdom Business Network are encouraged to view their businesses and professional relationships as platforms for ministry. This involves ethical business operations, fostering environments where Christian values are upheld, and actively seeking opportunities to share the Gospel with clients, employees, and peers in a manner that is both respectful and contextually appropriate. The network facilitates connections among Christian business owners, enabling them to support one another and collaborate in their evangelistic efforts.

The impact of KBN extends beyond individual businesses, influencing the broader market and community through the demonstration of Kingdom principles in action. By prioritizing integrity, generosity, and servant leadership, businesses within the network often stand out, drawing attention to the difference that Christian faith makes in the competitive world of commerce. This not only opens doors for conversations about faith but also showcases the transformative power of the Gospel in personal and corporate life.

Through workshops, resources, and networking events, KBN equips its members with the skills and knowledge necessary to effectively merge their entrepreneurial endeavors with their spiritual calling. This synergy between faith and work exemplifies the essence of Marketplace Evangelism, proving that the workplace and the marketplace are indeed ripe fields for sowing the seeds of the Gospel.

For more information and to join
Kingdom Business Network, go to:
www.kingdombusinessnetwork.com

Stable Churches Engage in Evangelistic Outreach

A church cannot accurately represent the kingdom of God alone. A stable church must engage in evangelistic outreach, both within its community and beyond. When a church is committed to spreading the Gospel message, it becomes a powerful force for transformation in its surrounding area. This transformation occurs not only through physical, tangible acts of service but also through the spiritual influence that comes from sharing the Gospel.

Churches that excel in evangelistic outreach are intentional and strategic in their efforts. They make it a priority to consistently communicate the message of salvation, not only through events and programs but also through personal interactions and relationships. These churches understand that evangelism is not a one-time event but an ongoing process of building trust, speaking truth, and demonstrating love.

Moreover, stable churches recognize that evangelism is not

limited to preaching and teaching but also involves serving and ministering to the needs of their community. This could include partnering with local organizations, providing practical assistance, or simply being a source of hope and compassion for those in need. By actively engaging in the lives of those around them, these churches demonstrate the love of Christ in tangible ways, making the message of salvation even more impactful.

In addition, stable churches prioritize equipping their members to share their faith effectively. This involves creating a culture of evangelism within the church and providing resources and training for individuals to confidently share their personal experiences with God's love and grace. By empowering their members to become ambassadors for Christ, these churches not only increase their impact but also fulfill the Great Commission in a meaningful and authentic way.

Marketplace Evangelism and evangelistic outreach are vital components of fulfilling the Great Commission. Whether through personal interactions, professional networks, or intentional community engagement, we are called to spread the message of salvation wherever we go. By seizing opportunities and stepping out in faith, we can make a lasting impact on our world for the glory of God.

The Church Continued in Sound Doctrine

The early church's unwavering steadfastness and remarkable stability were profoundly evident in its wholehearted commitment to sound doctrine. The apostles, understanding the pivotal role of doctrine, placed an extraordinary emphasis on teaching and steadfastly upholding the fundamental truths of the Christian faith. They ensured that believers were not merely acquainted with, but stood firm in their understanding and application of God's Word.

This rigorous focus on doctrine is undeniably essential for the health, unity, and growth of any church, as it serves as a bulwark against the insidious creep of false teachings and ensures that the congregation is deeply rooted in truth, fostering a community of believers who are well-equipped to navigate challenges to their faith.

In today's rapidly changing world, characterized by an incessant influx of information and a myriad of divergent ideas, the importance of maintaining a steadfast commitment to sound doctrine cannot be overstated for contemporary churches. This unwavering adherence not only acts as a protective shield, guarding believers from being led astray by the alluring yet deceptive philosophies of the age but also empowers them to engage effectively in evangelism. They become adept at sharing the Gospel with clarity and conviction, addressing the misconceptions or questions about Christianity that are prevalent in today's society. Moreover, in an era that increasingly values relativism and elevates personal opinions above absolute truth, the church's steadfast adherence to sound doctrine stands as a luminous testimony to the constancy of God's word and the unchanging character of His divine nature. It underscores the church's role as a beacon of truth in a world adrift in a sea of subjectivity, illuminating the path to salvation through Jesus Christ and fostering a deep, enduring faith among believers.

The Church Continued in Fellowship and Prayer

Another crucial aspect of the early church's stability was their commitment to fellowship and prayer. Acts 2:42 highlights that,

"they continued steadfastly in the apostles' doctrine, and fellowship, and in breaking of bread, and in prayers."

This emphasis on fellowship within the Body of Christ is essential for building community, providing support and encouragement, and fostering spiritual growth. Prayer, both individual and corporate, was also a significant aspect of the early church's steadfastness. It served as a constant reminder of their dependence on God and His power to sustain them through challenges and trials.

For the modern-day church, fellowship and prayer are just as vital for maintaining stability and effectively carrying out evangelistic outreach. It is through genuine relationships with other believers and a deep connection with God that we are equipped to boldly share the Gospel in our communities.

As Christians, we should strive for this same type of steadfastness and dedication in our lives and churches. By remaining rooted in sound doctrine, committed to fellowship and prayer, and persevering through challenges, we can embody the unchanging faithfulness of God and effectively carry out His mission of reaching the lost with the message of salvation.

The Church Continued in the Breaking of Bread and in Prayers

The early church's steadfastness and unwavering commitment were profoundly demonstrated through their dedication to the breaking of bread and engaging in fervent prayers. This phrase is rich in meaning, encapsulating both the sacred act of communion, or the Lord's Supper, and the consistent gatherings dedicated to prayer. Far from being mere rituals or empty traditions, these spiritual disciplines were foundational practices that served as powerful, tangible reminders of Christ's ultimate sacrifice on the cross and our deep need for continual dependence on Him for spiritual nourishment and strength.

In the contemporary context, it appears that many modern churches have drifted away from valuing the profound significance of these ancient, spiritual practices. Instead, there is an increasing tendency to prioritize programs, events, and activities that, while beneficial in some respects, may inadvertently shift the focus away from the core of Christian faith and fellowship. This shift can lead to a spiritual disconnect, where the essence of being part of the Body of Christ is diluted by the allure of busyness and church branding.

However, there is a beautiful opportunity for renewal and deep spiritual growth when we, as believers, choose to reaffirm our commitment to these foundational practices of breaking bread and engaging in communal prayers. By doing so, we not only honor the traditions handed down by the early church but also invite a refreshing of our faith and a deepening of our personal and communal relationship with God. These acts of worship and devotion are not just historical footnotes but are vibrant expressions of our collective faith and dependence on the Lord.

Moreover, these spiritual disciplines offer invaluable opportunities for believers to come together in unity, transcending denominational lines and cultural differences, thereby strengthening the fabric of the Body of Christ. In a world that is increasingly fragmented and isolated, the intentional gathering of believers to break bread in remembrance of Christ's sacrifice and to unite in prayer is a powerful testimony of our shared faith and the hope that we have in Jesus.

In embracing these practices with renewed focus and sincerity, we stand to not only enrich our individual spiritual journeys but also to foster a sense of belonging and community within the church. It is through these sacred practices that we are reminded of the love, sacrifice, and hope that binds us together as followers of Christ.

Spirit-Empowered Evangelism

Finally, in its steadfast commitment to sound doctrine, fellowship, and spiritual practices such as breaking of bread and prayer, the early church was also marked by a boldness and fervency in sharing the Gospel. Acts 4:31 describes how "they were all filled with the Holy Spirit, and they spoke the word of God with boldness." This empowerment by the Holy Spirit was crucial for the early church's effective evangelism, and it remains just as vital for believers today.

The Holy Spirit empowers us with boldness, wisdom, and discernment to effectively share the Gospel with those around us. It also enables us to overcome any fear or hesitation we may have in sharing our faith. As we continue in fellowship and prayer, seeking the guidance and empowerment of the Holy Spirit, we can become powerful agents for spreading the good news of salvation through Jesus Christ.

If one thing is evident in the book of Acts, it is that the remarkable vitality of the early churches was due to the supernatural power of the Holy Spirit. As believers, we must earnestly seek the continual filling of the Holy Spirit to carry out God's mission and share the love of Christ with others.

The steadfastness and stability of the early church were a result of their unwavering commitment to sound doctrine, fellowship, prayer, and spirit-empowered evangelism. These foundational practices are just as relevant and necessary for the modern-day church to thrive and effectively carry out its mission.

In the heart of genuine evangelism lies a profound, often overlooked truth: it's not just about disseminating sound theology but about sharing from a place of deep compassion and empathy. This principle isn't new; it traces back to centuries past, where figures like Jeremiah exemplified what it means to have a heart utterly broken for others. Jeremiah, in his time, wept bitterly over the sins of Israel, a nation straying far from its divine path. His cries,

"Is it nothing to you, all you who pass by?" (Lamentations 1:12)

echoed with a pain born of witnessing his people's rebellion against God. His tears (Lamentations 1:16) were not just for the sin but for the sinner, a distinction that reflects a profound understanding and empathy.

This concept of empathetic evangelism isn't confined to the Old Testament. Jesus Christ Himself, overlooking Jerusalem, wept (Luke 19:41). Imagine that scene—standing on a hill, gazing upon a city rich in spiritual heritage yet blinded by unbelief and rebellion. Why did He weep? Because His preaching was not just a duty but an outpouring of love for a lost populace, resistant to the message of hope and salvation He offered. His heartbreak over their spiritual state is a powerful reminder of the essence of true evangelism.

Evangelist Jonathan Edwards

Jonathan Edwards, a prominent figure in the First Great Awakening, delivered the sermon "Sinners in the Hands of an Angry God" with a fervor and intensity that echoed the deep, empathetic concern for the eternal state of his listeners. This sermon, known for its vivid imagery and impassioned plea, aimed to awaken and spur the congregation to repentance and recognition of their precarious standing before a just and holy God. Edwards' delivery, underscored by a profound burden for souls, led to an unprecedented response; the air was thick with weeping and cries for mercy as the weight of their sin and the reality of

God's imminent judgment became palpably clear to those in attendance.

His message, while stark, was imbued with a fatherly concern for the salvation of his listeners. It's crucial to note that the visceral reactions—tears, trembling, and vociferous pleas for forgiveness—were the fruits of genuine conviction and sorrow for sin. This deep response highlighted a collective yearning for redemption and a keen awareness of the gravity of their estrangement from God.

Edwards' sermon remains a landmark moment in religious history, not solely for its rhetorical power but for its capacity to drive individuals to a place of sincere repentance and spiritual renewal. Through his preaching, Edwards underscored the urgency of reconciliation with God and the profound mercy available through Christ. In doing so, "Sinners in the Hands of an Angry God" serves as a poignant reminder of the necessity of heartfelt repentance and the profound impact of empathetic evangelism.

Today, we're called to reflect on this model of evangelism—a model rooted not in judgment but in genuine concern and love for those around us. It's a wake-up call to move beyond the confines of clinical, detached approaches to sharing faith. The question then becomes, are we willing to allow our hearts to be so touched by the lives of others that we, too, can feel the weight of their spiritual journeys? Are we prepared to shed tears, to get on our knees in prayer, interceding for those who haven't yet found their way to God?

This is not about adopting a somber outlook on life but about awakening a fervent, passionate commitment to see change in the world, one soul at a time. It's about letting our hearts be so moved by compassion that our evangelism becomes more than just words —it becomes a reflection of God's own heart for His children.

If our Lord wept over the lost, we too should feel compelled to view evangelism through the lens of love and compassion. It's a call to action, urging us to embody the kind of evangelism that resonates with the heart of God—a heart that aches for every lost soul and rejoices over each one found. This perspective transforms our approach from mere duty to heartfelt devotion, from dry-eyed routine to a passionate plea for souls. In doing so, we not only follow in the footsteps of great prophets and our Savior but also align our efforts with the very heart of God's love and redemption for the lost in our world today.

Chapter 10

Building, Mending, and Closing The Net

The metaphor of being "Fishers of Men" finds its origins in the New Testament, where Jesus calls upon His first disciples, Simon Peter and Andrew, with a compelling mission statement:

"Follow me, and I will make you fishers of men."

This charge, recorded in the Gospel of Matthew (4:19), encapsulates the transformational call to discipleship. The essence of this metaphor is deeply rooted in the Jewish fishing culture, symbolizing the transition from a literal occupation to a spiritual vocation.

The significance of this metaphor extends beyond its initial context, serving as a call to all who would follow Jesus to engage in the work of spreading His teachings and gathering people into the fold of faith. In essence, "Fishers of Men" is a poetic depiction of evangelism, where the act of fishing mirrors the disciples' mission to reach out to the various "fish" in the sea of humanity, drawing them towards salvation and spiritual rebirth.

In the broader scriptural narrative, this metaphor is indicative of the inclusive and expansive nature of Jesus' ministry. Just as fishermen cast wide nets to gather fish of all kinds, so too are followers of Jesus encouraged to reach out to all individuals, regardless of their background or social standing, in the spirit of love and compassion. This approach emphasizes the universality of the Christian message and the fundamental belief in the potential for redemption and transformation in every human being.

The Importance of Working Together

Denominations have too long fragmented the unity of God's followers. While God can indeed operate within these divisions, members of any denomination should recognize that they are merely one vessel in a vast ocean. A narrow focus, denominational pride, and attitudes of detachment are not reflective of Christ's teachings. God's calling for us is to collaborate, which demands both humility and a spirit of cooperation.

When Jesus called Peter and Andrew to be "Fishers of Men," He did not ask them to work alone but instead invited them into a community of believers. Similarly, as modern-day followers of Christ, we are also called to work together in unity and harmony, casting our nets wide to reach as many people as possible.

In the journey of faith, it is crucial to remember that we are not alone. Just as fishermen support and assist each other in their work, so too should followers of Christ come together in fellowship, prayer, and service to fulfill the mission of being "Fishers of Men." This unity allows for collective strength, wisdom, and resources to be used for the greater good.

Moreover, working together as a united body of believers is not only beneficial to spreading the message of Christ but also for building and strengthening our own faith. When we come together, we are exposed to different perspectives, experiences, and insights. This can deepen our understanding of God's teachings and strengthen our relationship with Him.

In addition, collaboration among different denominations can help break down barriers and promote understanding and respect among God's followers. It allows us to see the common ground we share in our faith, rather than focusing on differences.

As Christians, it is essential to remember that we are all part of the same body, with Christ as our head. We should strive for unity and work together towards a shared goal of spreading His love and teachings to all corners of the globe. Together, we can achieve much more than we could ever do alone. Let us embrace our diversity and come together in harmony to fulfill God's calling for His followers.

Mending the Net

In the process of living out our lives there are times when we must mend, or repair, broken relationships. This requires humility, forgiveness, and a willingness to seek reconciliation.

As followers of Christ, we are called to be peacemakers and ambassadors of God's love. When conflicts arise within our communities, it is our duty to work towards healing and restoration. This may involve setting aside personal pride and grievances, and extending forgiveness and grace to others.

Furthermore, mending broken relationships within the Church is crucial for fulfilling the mission of being "Fishers of Men." When there is unity and harmony among believers, we can more effectively reach out to those who are lost or searching for spiritual guidance. Our actions and attitudes towards one another can be a powerful witness to non-believers, demonstrating the love and compassion of Christ.

> *"That there should be no schism in the body; but that the members should have the same care one for another. 26 And whether one member suffer, all the members suffer with it; or one member be honoured, all the members rejoice with it. 27 Now ye are the body of Christ, and members in particular."* ~ 1 Corinthians 12:25-27

Seeking Forgiveness and Reconciliation

Jesus teaches us the importance of seeking forgiveness from those we have wronged, and offering forgiveness to those who have wronged us. This is an essential part of mending broken relationships within our communities.

> *"For if ye forgive men their trespasses, your heavenly Father will also forgive you: 15 But if ye forgive not men their trespasses, neither will your Father forgive your trespasses."* ~ Matthew 6:14-15

Many like to quote Mark 11:22-24 and talk about having faith in God, believing and confessing etc., but verses 25-26 are all part of that same context.

> *"And when ye stand praying, forgive, if ye have ought against any: that your Father also which is in heaven may forgive you your trespasses. 26 But if ye do not forgive, neither will your Father which is in heaven forgive your trespasses."* ~ Mark 11:25-26

As followers of Christ, we must remember that forgiveness and reconciliation are not easy tasks. But through the guidance and strength of God, we can mend broken relationships and work towards a more unified body of believers. Let us follow in Jesus' footsteps and strive for love, unity, and forgiveness within our communities.

Collaborative Community Efforts to Reach the Unchurched and Lost

Local churches can enhance their outreach and impact within their communities through a variety of collaborative efforts. Joining forces not only pools resources but also demonstrates a powerful message of unity among believers. Here are some initiatives that can be undertaken collectively:

- **Community Service Projects:** Engage in hands-on service projects like feeding the homeless, neighborhood cleanups, and assisting the elderly. These projects meet tangible needs and open doors for spiritual conversations.

- **Joint Worship Services and Prayer Meetings:** Organize ecumenical services that bring different congregations together for worship and prayer. Such events can be especially impactful during significant Christian seasons like Easter and Christmas.

- **Sports Leagues and Family Fun Days:** Host community-wide sports events or family fun days as a neutral ground for building relationships and sharing the love of Christ in a non-threatening way.

- **Educational Workshops and Seminars:** Offer workshops on practical life skills, mental health support, or marriage and parenting seminars. These events can address real community needs while providing a platform for spiritual guidance.

- **Youth and Children's Camps:** Run inter-church camps and Vacation Bible Schools (VBS) for children and youth. These programs can be an effective way to engage with young people and introduce them to the Christian faith.

- **Outreach Concerts and Art Events:** Utilize music, art, and culture to create engaging events that can attract those outside the church. Collaborating on such events can bring a diversity of talents and resources together.

- **Disaster Response Teams:** Form joint church groups trained to respond in times of natural disasters or crises. Providing practical and emotional support during difficult times can open hearts to the gospel message.

- **Health Clinics and Blood Drives:** Collaborate to offer free health screenings, blood drives, or health education seminars. Showing care for physical well-being can lead to opportunities for spiritual care and conversation.

- **Literacy Programs and Educational Support:** Partner to offer tutoring or literacy classes for adults and children. Education is a powerful tool for community upliftment and provides a platform for building relationships.

- **Interfaith Dialogues:** While maintaining theological differences, churches can jointly host discussions with other faith communities to promote understanding and peace in the community.

These collaborative efforts not only amplify the churches' reach but also visibly manifest the unity and love among believers, drawing others to explore the source of this love and harmony.

Closing the Net

Closing the net is a powerful concept that occurs when various ministries collaborate closely, aligning their efforts harmoniously towards the shared objective of bringing lost souls to Christ. This collaborative spirit is not just about working in isolation but involves a concerted effort where everyone plays a part in the evangelistic process. When we pray with individuals, encouraging them to commit their lives to Christ, and simultaneously gather their contact information for follow-up purposes, we set the stage for a deeper engagement through discipleship training. This process of discipleship is crucial because it marks the beginning of a new believer's spiritual journey, offering them the guidance, support, community, and education they need to grow in their faith. Closing the net, therefore, is about much more than just the initial act of conversion; it's about nurturing a sustained and meaningful relationship with Christ, facilitated by the collective efforts of the church's ministries working in unison.

* * *

In conclusion, the acts of building, mending, and closing the net are profound illustrations of how we, as the body of Christ, can effectively engage with and positively impact our communities. From understanding the imperative nature of forgiveness and reconciliation to the strategic mobilization of community outreach efforts, and ultimately, ensuring the thorough discipleship of new believers, our mission is multifaceted. It commands a concerted effort that not only focuses on the initial act of evangelism but emphasizes the cultivation of a nurturing environment that supports spiritual growth and maturity. These endeavors, though challenging, are immensely rewarding and are central to the mission Christ has entrusted to his Church.

As we reflect on our roles within this divine mandate, it becomes clear that our collective efforts in building, mending, and closing the net are not mere tasks but are, in fact, vital expressions of our faith and obedience to the Great Commission. It requires of us a commitment to unity, a heart for service, and an unwavering trust in God's leading and provision. Through these actions, we bear witness to the transforming power of the Gospel and God's relentless love for humanity. May we proceed with a renewed sense of purpose and an invigorated passion to see lives changed, relationships restored, and communities revitalized in the name of Jesus Christ.

May I Introduce You to Jesus?

Are you feeling lost, searching for a purpose in life? Do you feel that something is missing, and you are not sure what it is? Do you want to know more about Jesus and the Bible? If yes, then you are in the right place. In this chapter, we will explore what a relationship with Jesus can mean for your life and eternity. The Bible says that when we come to Jesus, we receive spiritual rebirth, the forgiveness of sins, and eternal life. Let's talk about it.

The Biblical Basis for Coming to Jesus

God has provided us with precise instructions on how to come to Him through His Word, the Bible. Our first step is acknowledging our sins. Romans 3:23 says,

> *"For all have sinned and fall short of the glory of God."*

Therefore, we must recognize that we cannot save ourselves

with our own efforts. However, Jesus can save us, and we must believe in Him to receive salvation.

Acceptance and belief in His Word affect our lives in many ways. John 1:12 says,

> *"Yet to all who did receive him, to those who believed in his name, he gave the right to become children of God."*

By accepting Jesus into our lives, we gain the privilege of being God's children, and this changes our identity. We will have a new purpose in life and a new perspective on our struggles. We will experience forgiveness, acceptance, divine love, and the joy of living for God daily.

The Cross of Calvary reveals the ultimate sacrifice of Jesus Christ for our sins. Romans 5:8 says,

> *"But God demonstrates his love for us in this: While we were still sinners, Christ died for us."*

Jesus paid the price for our sins, and we can receive forgiveness and salvation through Him. It is through His death and resurrection that we can come to the Father and receive the Holy Spirit.

As humans, we all have our shortcomings and faults. No one is perfect, and that's why we need Jesus in our lives. Romans 6:23 states,

> *"For the wages of sin is death; but the gift of God is eternal life through Jesus Christ our Lord."*

It's a beautiful thing to know that there's a way out of the darkness, and that's through Jesus Christ. Its not an easy decision to make, but its a crucial one that we all must make if we want to experience true freedom and life. So, if you're feeling lost and hopeless today, know that there's hope in Jesus. He's waiting with open arms to welcome you into His love and grace.

Praying a prayer of salvation is a simple and powerful step toward salvation. We must confess our faith and ask for forgiveness of our sins. Romans 10:9 says,

"If you declare with your mouth, Jesus is Lord, and believe in your heart that God raised him from the dead, you will be saved."

The following is a simple prayer guide:

Dear Lord Jesus,

I know that I am a sinner and that I cannot save myself. I believe that you died on the Cross for my sins and that you rose again. Please forgive me of my sins and come into my heart. Right now, I confess and receive You as my Lord and Savior. Thank you for giving me eternal life. In Jesus' name, Amen.

What Now?

Congratulations on your decision to follow Jesus Christ and join the family of God! You are no longer alone in your journey of faith. It's exciting to think about the wonderful things God has in store for you as you grow and mature in Him. Whether you are new to Christianity or have walked with the Lord for a while, this guide will help you navigate the ups and downs of your faith journey.

Being a part of the Family of God is a rich and rewarding experience that comes with responsibilities and opportunities. Now that you have received salvation, you have the privilege of being called a child of God. The concept of having a personal relationship with Jesus Christ must be taken seriously, as it is an ongoing process if one is to continuously grow in their faith.

Daily Prayer

The first step is to understand the power of prayer. Prayer is a conversation with God that helps establish and strengthen an intimate relationship with Him. Cultivate the habit of prayer by setting aside a specific time each day to talk with God. One of the most important components of prayer is learning how to listen to what God is trying to say. Many people think that prayer is constantly talking to God. May I encourage you that prayer is one part talking and two parts listening. Just look in the mirror; we all have one mouth and two ears.

Praying daily is a wonderful way to connect with God's heart and deepen your relationship with Him. It allows for open communication so that you can share your thoughts, feelings, and aspirations with Him. You may also take this time to thank Him for your blessings and ask for His guidance in making decisions. With each prayer, you build a stronger connection with God and can find peace knowing that He is always there to listen and support you.

Throughout the years, many people have asked me,

"How can I hear God's voice?"

My answer to them has consistently been,

"If we sit in His presence, we can learn His voice."

God speaks to everyone differently. He wants to have an active relationship "with you, and the best way to do this is through communication. One of the ways that God has communicated to us is through His Word.

Daily Bible Reading

Reading the Bible is an incredible way to receive guidance on God's will for your life. The Bible contains gems of wisdom and encouragement that can help us navigate the twists and turns of life. Whether we're facing a tough decision, feeling lost or simply seeking direction, the Bible is a faithful companion that provides solid, reliable advice. What's more, the Bible is a gift that strengthens our relationship with God. Through reading its pages, we can learn about His character, understand His love and gain a deeper appreciation of His goodness. Reading the Bible isn't just about finding direction - its about drawing closer to the One who created us and has a hope-filled plan for our lives.

To grow in faith and knowledge, one must engage in daily bible reading and study. The Bible is the guidebook that reveals who God is, what He has done, and what He expects of us. In addition to personal bible reading, its important to receive sound teaching through fellowship with other believers. It's helpful to attend small groups, Sunday services, and listen to online messages. With practice, the things you learn will become deeply rooted in your heart and transform your life.

Christian Friends

Finding Christian friends is also essential to your growth in faith. When you're immersed in a community of believers, you have the opportunity to build deep, authentic relationships. These relationships build support and accountability, which will help you stay on the right path. Connecting with a church community is vital to your spiritual growth. A church provides a place where you can worship God in community, hear the Word preached, and serve the body of Christ.

Being part of a church provides not only solid teaching but a community of like-minded believers that share a common faith. There is nothing quite like experiencing the joy of fellowship with others who are seeking to grow in their relationship with God. You'll find people who come from all walks of life, with different backgrounds and experiences but united in a common goal - to know and love God more deeply. As you sit under the teaching of pastors and teachers, you'll discover a depth to your faith that you never thought possible. Through worship, prayer, and study of the Bible, you'll feel your heart expanding with an overwhelming sense of gratitude and thankfulness for all that God is doing in your life. Truly, belonging to a church is an experience that is both fulfilling and life-changing.

Developing a Servants Heart

Putting your learning into practice through the practical application of your faith is an important step in growth. Serving others is one way to do so. Jesus spent His life serving others and has called us to do the same. Jesus' example reminds us that we need to get outside of our comfort zones and bless others with our time, energy, and resources. Volunteer at church, donate to a charity, or work in your community. With time, as you serve and bless others, you'll find that God is guiding and shaping you into a better version of yourself.

Living Grateful

Living a life that is grateful, faithful, and holy is truly a blessing. As we honor God in all areas of our lives, we can't help but feel an overwhelming sense of joy and fulfillment. It's not always the easiest path to take, but when we choose to put our trust in Him and seek His will for our lives, we can rest assured that we are on the right track. When we live with gratitude in our hearts, we begin to see the world in a different light, and our relationships with others are strengthened. Ultimately, living a life that honors God is the best decision we can make, and we can trust that He will guide us every step of the way.

Pride and gratitude cannot co-exist. Rejoicing in the blessings of salvation is the ultimate goal of every Christian. It's easy to get bogged down in day-to-day challenges that we forget to celebrate the victory we have in Jesus. To celebrate the goodness of God, it's essential to practice gratitude. Remember that your salvation is a free gift from God that you didn't deserve, and nothing you do can take it away. Celebrate divine love, mercy, and grace by sharing joyful testimonies with others. Encourage others with your story and how God has changed your life.

Welcome to the Family!

About the Author

For more information on Dr. Jonathan Vorce just go to
www.about.me/jonathanvorce

Affordable | Accessible | Accredited | Online

Dr. Vorce is the Chancellor of Covenant University, Inc. Degrees range from first year through Ph.D.

More information is available on our website:
www.covenantuniversityonline.com

Also by Jonathan Vorce

Presence Driven

Hosting the Holy Ghost

Christian Leadership

Building Successful Ministry

Shepherding in the 21st Century

Kingdom Economics

Divine Authority

The Ministry of Presence (Chaplaincy)

Non-Profit Creation and Management

All books may be ordered on Amazon.com and most online places where books are sold.

Made in the USA
Columbia, SC
29 May 2024

36003406R10109